Black/White Relations
in American History

THE MAGILL BIBLIOGRAPHIES

The American Presidents, by Norman S. Cohen, 1989
Black American Women Novelists, by Craig Werner, 1989
Classical Greek and Roman Drama, by Robert J. Forman, 1989
Contemporary Latin American Fiction, by Keith H. Brower, 1989
Masters of Mystery and Detective Fiction, by J. Randolph Cox, 1989
Nineteenth Century American Poetry, by Philip K. Jason, 1989
Restoration Drama, by Thomas J. Taylor, 1989
Twentieth Century European Short Story, by Charles E. May, 1989
The Victorian Novel, by Laurence W. Mazzeno, 1989
Women's Issues, by Laura Stempel Mumford, 1989
America in Space, by Russell R. Tobias, 1991
The American Constitution, by Robert J. Janosik, 1991
The Classical Epic, by Thomas J. Sienkewicz, 1991
English Romantic Poetry, by Bryan Aubrey, 1991
Ethics, by John K. Roth, 1991
The Immigrant Experience, by Paul D. Mageli, 1991
The Modern American Novel, by Steven G. Kellman, 1991
Native Americans, by Frederick E. Hoxie and Harvey Markowitz, 1991
American Drama: 1918-1960, by R. Baird Shuman, 1992
American Ethnic Literatures, by David R. Peck, 1992
American Theatre History, by Thomas J. Taylor, 1992
The Atomic Bomb, by Hans G. Graetzer and Larry M. Browning, 1992
Biography, by Carl Rollyson, 1992
The History of Science, by Gordon L. Miller, 1992
The Origin and Evolution of Life on Earth, by David W. Hollar, 1992
Pan-Africanism, by Michael W. Williams, 1992
Resources for Writers, by R. Baird Shuman, 1992
Shakespeare, by Joseph Rosenblum, 1992
The Vietnam War in Literature, by Philip K. Jason, 1992
Contemporary Southern Women Fiction Writers, by Rosemary M. Canfield Reisman and Christopher J. Canfield, 1994
Cycles in Humans and Nature, by John T. Burns, 1994
Environmental Studies, by Diane M. Fortner, 1994
Poverty in America, by Steven Pressman, 1994
The Short Story in English: Britain and North America, by Dean Baldwin and Gregory L. Morris, 1994

Victorian Poetry, by Laurence W. Mazzeno, 1995

Human Rights in Theory and Practice, by Gregory J. Walters, 1995

Energy, by Joseph R. Rudolph, Jr., 1995

A Bibliographic History of the Book, by Joseph Rosenblum, 1995

The Search for Economics as a Science, by the Editors of Salem Press (Lynn Turgeon, Consulting Editor), 1995

Psychology, by the Editors of Salem Press (Susan E. Beers, Consulting Editor), 1995

World Mythology, by Thomas J. Sienkewicz, 1996

Art, Truth, and High Politics: A Bibliographic Study of the Official Lives of Queen Victoria's Ministers in Cabinet, 1843-1969, by John Powell, 1996

Popular Physics and Astronomy, by Roger Smith, 1996

Paradise Lost, by P. J. Klemp, 1996

Social Movement Theory and Research, by Roberta Garner and John Tenuto, 1996

Propaganda in Twentieth Century War and Politics, by Robert Cole, 1996

The Kings of Medieval England, c. 560-1485, by Larry W. Usilton, 1996

The British Novel 1680-1832, by Laurence W. Mazzeno, 1997

The Impact of Napoleon, 1800-1815, by Leigh Ann Whaley, 1997

Cosmic Influences on Humans, Animals, and Plants, by John T. Burns, 1997

One Hundred Years of American Women Writing, 1848-1948, by Jane Missner Barstow, 1997

Vietnam Studies, by Carl Singleton, 1997

British Women Writers, 1700-1850, by Barbara J. Horwitz, 1997

The United States and Latin America, by John A. Britton, 1997

Reinterpreting Russia, by Steve D. Boilard, 1997

Theories of Myth, by Thomas J. Sienkewicz, 1997

Women and Health, by Frances R. Belmonte, 1997

Contemporary Southern Men Fiction Writers, by Rosemary M. Canfield Reisman and Suzanne Booker-Canfield, 1998

Black/White Relations in American History, by Leslie V. Tischauser, 1998

The Creation/Evolution Controversy, by James L. Hayward, 1998

The Beat Generation, by William Lawlor, 1998

Biographies of Scientists, by Roger Smith, 1998

Introducing Canada, by Brian Gobbett and Robert Irwin, 1998

Four British Women Novelists: Anita Brookner, Margaret Drabble, Iris Murdoch, Barbara Pym, by George Soule, 1998

Black/White Relations in American History

An Annotated Bibliography

Leslie V. Tischauser

Magill Bibliographies

The Scarecrow Press, Inc.
Lanham, Md., & London
and
Salem Press
Pasadena, Calif., & Englewood Cliffs, N.J.
1998

SCARECROW PRESS, INC.

Published in the United States of America
by Scarecrow Press, Inc.
4720 Boston Way
Lanham, Maryland 20706

4 Pleydell Gardens, Folkestone
Kent CT20 2DN, England

British Library Cataloguing in Publication Information Available

Library of Congress Cataloging-in-Publication Data

Tischauser, Leslie Vincent, 1942–
    Black/white relations in American history : an annotated
bibliography / Leslie V. Tischauser.
        p.   cm. — (The Magill bibliographies)
    Includes indexes.
    ISBN 0-8108-3389-1 (alk. paper)
    1. United States—Race relations—Bibliography. 2. Afro
-Americans—Civil rights—History—Bibliography. I. Title.
II. Series.
Z1361.N39T57 1998
[E185.61]
016.3058'00973—dc21   98-3158
                              CIP

Contents

Acknowledgments

I would like to express my gratitude for assistance to the librarians and staff of the University of Illinois, Chicago, where most of this work was done, and at Prairie State Community College, Chicago Heights, Illinois. I would also like to thank Professor Numan Bartley for expanding my interest in this topic during a seminar he devoted to this topic many years ago. Michael Perman has also been instrumental in inspiring me to complete this work. Patrick Faulkner and Walter Kuhn are two other colleagues who have shared their views and wisdom with me over time. Without the help, faith, and interest of my wife, Connie, this volume would never have been completed. Thanks to you all.

INTRODUCTION

In his Second Inaugural Address, President Bill Clinton called race the "constant curse" of American society. This bibliography shows how the question of black/white has always been a terrible problem for Americans, from the first time a slave ship landed at Jamestown in 1619 to the Rodney King riots and church-burnings of the 1990's. In the following pages, I have attempted to list the key historical and sociological treatments of the topic of race relations that have been published since 1945. It is hoped that students, teachers, and researchers can use this bibliography as a guide and that it can help them find the best books available on the area of black/white relations they are studying. Black/white relations, rather than race relations, have been emphasized. Throughout American history, it has been the connections between those two groups that have served as the model for associations between other groups. How whites have treated African Americans has set the standard for dealing with other minority groups.

Chapter 1 includes the major works on the theory, history, and science of race and race relations published since the end of World War II. The chapter describes the most recent works defining the scientific concept of race and the most significant interpretations of how people treat each other because of racial distinctions. Race is a scientific term based on differences in blood types (and little else of any major scientific importance), while "race relations" refers to the ways people act and respond to each other on the basis of their perceived distinctions. The idea of race can be made very important or not significant at all depending on the attitudes, assumptions, and prejudices of people involved.

Chapter 2, "Slavery and Race," presents the major books on American slavery, its origins, development, and the changes in the institution over time. New World slavery differed from the kind of unfree labor found in most of the world chiefly because here it was based on skin color. Slaves in other areas of the world were usually prisoners of war or debtors. Racism, defined as hating another person because of skin color or false ideas about the meaning of race, lay at the heart of slavery in North America. Ideas of racial supremacy motivated slaveholders, who also made a good living by exploiting their slaves—economically, socially, and legally. The works described, many written in the 1960's and 1970's, the "Golden Age" of American slavery studies, are general surveys of the entire process of enslavement from the African background to the conditions found in cities and plantations in the United States.

Chapter 3 lists studies of slavery in specific states and localities. Many of these studies are concerned with how slaves interacted with other slaves and their masters. There are books on every region of the United States, including the North where slavery existed until after the American Revolution. There are also studies concerning slave families, religion, folklore, and culture. Other works in this chapter explain how American law, national, state, and constitutional, defended white supremacy and denied human and natural rights to African Americans, free or slave.

The status and condition of the "free black" portion of the African American community before the Civil War is the subject of chapter 4. Treatment of this group of free men was a true indicator of the amount of prejudice and discrimination faced by black citizens. Slaves were not citizens under the law, free blacks could have been if any idea of equality existed. Yet in the North as well as in the South, free blacks, who constituted about five percent of the African American population, faced endless hostility and rejection, not because they were slaves but because they were black. No matter where they lived they were considered to be at the bottom of the economic ladder. A few became successful, usually as barbers, caterers, or undertakers, but they were social outcasts and rejected by the white elite despite their wealth. Not even those very few free black families who adopted a major indicator of wealth and prosperity, their own slaves, could expect equal treatment from white people.

Chapter 4 also includes a description of studies of major slave revolts and other forms of resistance. These analyses show the difficulty of resistance because of the great advantages enjoyed by white society. Whites had all the guns, all the laws, and all the instruments of torture and terror on their side. Revolts and rebellions were dealt with violently, aggressively, and with a great deal of brutality. Punishment for rebels was swift, sure, and deadly. Whites feared a slave rebellion more than anything else, perhaps because they were sure that the first step after any successful revolt would be the killing of all whites in the area. The fear of race war and bloody retaliation played a major role in the South's steadfast refusal to end slavery, and in their later (successful) attempt to segregate society through law and terror.

The theories and defenses erected by whites to protect slavery and notions of racial superiority are examined in the books cited in chapter 5. Racist ideas were held not only by impoverished, illiterate, badly educated rural whites but also were openly expressed by the best and brightest white minds of the entire pre-Civil War period in the North and South. There was very little dissent on the question, whites were superior to other humans in all aspects of their being. These views were based on scientific investigations and, more important, on the religious beliefs of Americans. Racism unified white society. Whether rich, poor, or miserable, a white person could feel superior to the most successful African American.

Racism unified whites in a deadly alliance fighting against the feared ideal of equality, whether social, political, or economic. The amount of racist hostility expressed by whites was enormous. Almost all believed in the innate inferiority of black people, and even if some expressed a love for their slaves or black folks it was at best the love of a master for his dog.

Chapter 6 presents the major books dealing with the period of Reconstruction from 1865 to 1877, that brief era after the Civil War when some political leaders made an effort to resolve the problem of race relations at least in the South. History destroys the popular myth that white southerners were mistreated and abused by carpetbaggers and "Yankee invaders." The old picture of a defeated South further impoverished by Radical Republican extremists is difficult to erase, and many people still cling to it. Most recent interpretations of the period, however, point to exactly the opposite picture. Reconstruction was a violent period in the United States but the violence and terror came from the Ku Klux Klan and former Confederate soldiers who launched a successful and bloody campaign to restore white control of their states. Two societies, separate and unequal, emerged from the struggle. Former slaves were forced into separate economic and social communities and lost all political power, including the right to vote. Lynching played a major role in creating this New South, which was based on legal segregation and white supremacy.

Chapter 7 reviews the major books discussing lynching and racial violence in the South and the rest of the United States. Violence, or the threat of violence was at the core of black/white relations in American society. Not all young black males had to be tortured or mutilated by a lynch mob to send a message to the entire African American community: Stay in your place, do not challenge the system, or you will die. From 1885 to 1930, the United States averaged one or more lynchings every week. A culture of violence developed that protected a notion of white manhood through killing others.

The studies of racial segregation in chapter 8 generally conclude that separation by skin color has always been a part of American culture. Segregation by law did not begin in the 1880's, it began in the 1660's in Virginia with ratification of the first slave code and continued in the development of Black Codes in many northern states to deal with free blacks. Skin color has always been more important in holding together the white majority than any other factor, including social class, employment, politics, or patriotism. Industrialization did not change the pattern of race relations, North or South; it simply took place within the structures of racism. Urbanization did not change the ideas, principles, or values of white supremacy; it did, however, improve the quality of life for many blacks by offering them jobs, housing, and better educational opportunities, albeit in racist settings. None of these benefits were available in traditional, white-dominated, Southern rural counties. Unions were segregated, housing was segregated, transportation was segregated, and separate but equal facilities existed only in the minds of Supreme Court judges and other white citizens who refused to look at the reality of underfunding of black schools and the evils of legalizing prejudice. Yet, within the adverse conditions found in a racist society, black communities emerged and some flourished.

Chapters 9 and 10 describe the major interpretations of the origins of the Civil Rights movement and the fight against racism and legal segregation. The great migration to the North has also been much written about and the key works on this topic are also listed. Changes in black/white relations occurred because of economic depression, war, political leadership, Supreme Court decisions, and brave efforts to fight for equal rights under the Constitution. One thing became apparent, the fight for legal and political rights proceeded at a far faster rate than did the effort to change attitudes and fight racist ideas. That struggle has a much longer road to travel. Chapter 11 describes studies of the social, political, economic, and psychological costs of a nation's total history of racism, prejudice, and discrimination. The truly huge number of works available in this area has meant that only those found to be most important and easily available have been included.

Chapter 1

RACE AND RACE RELATIONS

GENERAL SURVEYS

Ackermann, Robert John. *Heterogeneities: Race, Gender, Class, Nation, and State*. Amherst: University of Massachusetts Press, 1996.
A philosopher offers his views of modern race relations. Racism becomes important in the life of a society when elite leaders give the signal that hating others is acceptable and that treating others differently because of the color of their skin is legitimate. 218 pages with an index.

Anderson, David D., and Robert L. Wright, eds. *The Dark and Tangled Path: Race in America*. Boston: Houghton Mifflin, 1971.
A collection of essays, speeches, short stories, and documents on race relations from the colonial period to the 1960's. Includes Cotton Mather on Indians, Thomas Jefferson on slavery, excerpts from the Lincoln-Douglas debates, Bret Harte's views on prejudice against Chinese, as well as several pictures and cartoons. 444 pages with an index.

Baker, John R. *Race*. New York: Oxford University Press, 1974.
A British scientist views modern theories of race and their significance. Evidence shows that no one can claim superiority because he or she belongs to a particular ethnic group. Skin color differences emerged in reaction to the rays of the sun; it has no other scientific importance. 625 pages with eighty-two illustrations, a bibliography, extensive notes, and an index. Complicated scientific discussions make this a difficult book for the general reader.

Banton, Michael. *The Idea of Race*. Boulder, Colo.: Westview Press, 1977.
An excellent source for summaries of the major sociological interpretations of race relations since the 1850's. Race relations is defined as the relations between groups who see each other as having clear differences based on skin color. Considers Joseph-Arthur de Gobineau, the Social Darwinists, Robert E. Park, W. Lloyd Warner, Gunnar

Myrdal, Theodor Adorno, and many others. 190 pages with a bibliography and an index.

Berry, Mary Frances. *Black Resistance/White Law: A History of Constitutional Racism in America.* Rev. ed. New York: Penguin, 1994.
Sees the law as the major instrument for maintaining racism in the United States. Laws have reflected the will of the white majority which seeks to keep blacks in a position of economic and social inferiority. Written by a member of the U.S. Civil Rights Commission, 1993-1994, who is also a lawyer and a professor of history. Includes chapters on lynchings, riots, and race inspired murders. A good place to start for a view of racism in American law. 319 pages, with an appendix containing excerpts from the U.S. Code, a bibliographical note, and an index.

Brooks, Roy L. *Rethinking the American Race Problem.* Berkeley: University of California Press, 1990.
Challenges strict focus on race as the key factor in minority relations. Suggests that the status of blacks is also a reflection of class distinctions. Whites will never help poor blacks. Calls for blacks to help themselves. No more waiting for government assistance. The government simply will never fulfill its promises. Middle-class blacks must begin a program of self-help to improve the lives of the urban underclass. 256 pages with a table of cases in civil rights law, extensive notes, a bibliography, and an index. The author is a professor of law.

Cox, Oliver Cromwell. *Caste, Class, and Race: A Study in Social Dynamics.* Garden City, N.Y.: Doubleday, 1948.
Presents an economic interpretation based on the author's Marxist views. The position of blacks is that of most exploited workers in a capitalist system. Race plays a major role in preventing white workers from seeing themselves in the same economic status. The false idea of racial superiority, perpetrated by the bourgeoisie, keeps white and black workers from seeing their common bond of exploitation.

_____. *Race Relations: Elements and Social Dynamics.* Detroit: Wayne State University Press, 1976.
The posthumously published views of a black Marxist sociologist. Discusses the economic causes of discrimination. The barriers to jobs and business opportunities due to racial repression and exclusion have severely limited the capacity of blacks to achieve equality. The alienated black population needs compensatory assistance or it will seek ways to make white society pay or suffer for past wrongs. 337 pages with five charts, forty tables, notes, and a brief bibliography.

Daniels, Roger, and Harry H. L. Kitano. *American Racism: Exploration of the Nature of Prejudice.* Englewood Cliffs, N.J.: Prentice-Hall, 1970.
A brief look at the history of discrimination against blacks, Japanese, Chinese, and Mexicans from 1769 to 1968. Prejudice, the prejudgment of others, can be prevented from spilling over into active discrimination and economic or psychological deprivation. But it takes great effort, endless attempts at education, and a major role for government in protecting the minority group from abuse. The costs of discrimination are quite high: health, education, manners and the morals of minorities are depressed while delinquency, criminality, and mental illness increase disproportionately. A brief book, 155 pages, with six documents and an index.

De Conde, Alexander. *Ethnicity, Race, and American Foreign Policy: A History.* Boston: Northeastern University Press, 1992.
Explores how and why ethnic groups and racial groups have influenced foreign policy in the United States. They have had greater influence, the author believes, than religion or social class. Begins with German and Irish influence on the American Revolution and concludes with Arab American reactions to the Gulf War of 1991. 270 pages with notes, a bibliography, and an index.

Franklin, John Hope. *Color and Race.* Boston: Houghton Mifflin, 1968.
Eighteen essays by historians and sociologists presented at the Conference on Race and Color at the University of California at Los Angeles (just a week before the 1965 Watts riot.) An introduction by the editor, the distinguished historian, provides a historical analysis of American race relations. Two essays are especially worth reading: Philip Mason's "The Revolt Against Western Values" (pages 50-74) and Kenneth J. Gergen's "The Significance of Skin Color in Human Relations" (pages 112-128). Other essays consider events in South Africa, India, and the West Indies. 391 pages with an index.

Franklin, Raymond S., and Solomon Resnik. *The Political Economy of Racism.* New York: Holt, Rinehart and Winston, 1973.
A general economic and political history of the problems of racism. Describes the historic legacy of racism, the economics of discrimination, the emergence of the ghetto, and the origins of social class and racial divisions. 279 pages with an index.

Frederickson, George M. *The Arrogance of Race: Historical Perspectives on Slavery, Racism, and Social Inequality.* Middletown, Conn.: Wesleyan University Press, 1988.

Seventeen essays on race relations in the United States and South Africa by one of the best historians writing on the subject. Racism in America grew stronger after the ending of slavery in 1865. Freedmen were a far greater threat to equality than were slaves. Race, rather than social class, has been the most important source of division in America. Yet, racism is not an incurable disease of human nature rooted deep in the psyche, but a product of historical circumstances, slavery and the fear of violence, as well as culture and politics. Hence, racism can be overcome only it would require a huge effort. 310 pages with extensive notes and an index.

Gossett, Thomas F. *Race: The History of an Idea in America.* Dallas: Southern Methodist University Press, 1965.
A professor of English presents an intellectual history of racist ideology from colonial times to 1960. Describes attitudes of American writers and scientific investigators toward blacks, Indians, Chinese, and European immigrants. Some writers eventually recognized that as a source of explanation for mental and temperamental traits race was worthless. For others, however, including literary naturalists such as Owen Wister, Jack London, and Frank Norris, racial distinctions still defined human beings. A lengthy 510 pages with an index. For another view, see William Stanton's *The Leopard's Spots*, cited below.

Harris, Marvin. *Patterns of Race Relations in America.* New York: Walker, 1964.
A brief anthropological view that challenges the idea that slaves were treated more kindly in the United States than in Brazil or other parts of South America. Presents a view of race relations that finds great inequality in North and South America. 154 pages with maps, pictures, a bibliography, and an index.

Hill, Herbert, and James E. Jones, Jr. *Race in America: The Struggle for Equality.* Madison: University of Wisconsin Press, 1993.
Sixteen essays from a 1989 conference celebrating the thirty-fifth anniversary of *Brown v. Board of Education of Topeka* (1954). Participants included federal judges, civil rights leaders, sociologists, psychologists, and historians. The most significant presentations were social psychologist Kenneth Clark's "Racial Progress and Retreat," on pages 3-18. Clark, who presented much of the evidence used by the Supreme Court in reaching its decision outlawing segregation makes keen observations on recent trends in American race relations. In "School Desegregation After Two Generations" (pages 234-262), so-

ciologist Gary Orfield challenges the view that desegregation had no impact on learning. Historian Ronald Takaki outlines reverses in race relations during two violent decades in "Race and Class in the 1880's and the 1980's" (pages 402-416). Other essays treat the legal background of the case and changes in the Court's view of equality of rights since 1954. 465 pages with notes and an index.

Hoetink, H. *Slavery and Race Relations in the Americas: Comparative Notes on Their Nature and Nexus.* New York: Harper & Row, 1973.
The pessimistic views of a Dutch sociologist. Every ethnic and racial group has a "somatic norm"—a conception of beauty unique to that group. Thus, every group is racist since the more others differ from the conception of perfection the more they are despised. Preference is always shown for persons who appear more like the ideal of beauty. Racism serves to preserve the dominance of the group in power. An important book that finds little hope for change. Racism is built into the human mind and the somatic norm is difficult to change. 232 pages with an index.

Jackson, Peter, ed. *Race and Racism: Essays in Social Geography.* London: Allen & Unwin, 1995.
Fourteen essays concerning race relations in England and the United States. Especially interesting is John Sick, "Racist and Anti-Racist Ideology in Films of the American South," pages 326-346, which includes a marvelous discussion of the making of the film *Gone with the Wind* (1939). 356 pages with an index.

Keyes, Alan L. *Masters of the Dream: The Strength and Betrayal of Black America.* New York: William Morrow, 1995.
The views of the conservative African American talk show host and presidential candidate. To Keyes, the American Dream is the "dream of freedom." African Americans showed their commitment to freedom by fighting against and rejecting slavery. Blacks should do no other than fight for what is right now, freedom from government control and welfare. 214 pages with an index.

Kousser, J. Morgan, and James C. McPherson, eds. *Region, Race, and Reconstruction: Essays in Honor of C. Vann Woodward.* New York: Oxford University Press, 1982.
Essays written to honor the leading historian of the New South concerning subjects from pro-slavery defense to the ending of Reconstruction. The best essay is Barbara J. Fields's "Ideology and Race in

American History," on pages 143-178. 463 pages with a bibliography of Woodward's contributions to history and an index.

Levine, Alan J. *Race Relations Within Western Expansion.* Westport, Conn.: Praeger, 1996.
A historian with a specialization in Russian society takes the long view on the subject of slavery and race. Attacks the view that previous generations should have had the same views of equality and justice that modern humanity has adopted. Slavery in its historical context has always existed, until at least the 1900's. It should be seen as part of many human societies not just Western. Attacks the view that differences are created by genetics rather than culture. Offers a useful perspective on the problems of race relations. 168 pages with a select bibliography and an index.

Lincoln, C. Eric. *Race, Religion, and the Continuing American Dilemma.* New York: Hill & Wang, 1984.
A collection of eight essays by a professor of religious and cultural studies. The best essay is "The Racial Factor in the Shaping of Religion in America" (pages 23-60). For racism to flourish as it does in the United States, there has to be a climate of acceptance. The religion of the white majority provides a rationale for white supremacy and has sacrificed its moral validity by supporting it. 282 pages with notes, a bibliography, and an index.

Lyman, Stanford M. *Color, Culture, Civilization: Race and Minority Issues in American Society.* Urbana: University of Illinois Press, 1994.
Explores the dynamics of the debate over pluralism and assimilation. Finds that currently assimilation as a model or explanation of American history is rejected in academic circles, yet it holds a wide attraction for the newer immigrant communities. An interesting view of theories of assimilation from Robert Park, who accepted the idea, to black economist Thomas Sowell, who talks about "inherited traits" among racial and ethnic groups and rejects assimilation. Interesting chapters on recent Asian, Indian, and Japanese immigrants. 398 pages with endnotes and an index.

Mack, Raymond W. *Race, Class, and Power.* 2d ed. New York: American Book Company, 1968.
A collection of essays by prominent sociologists originally published in professional journals. These essays support the idea of social stratification, that race relations is part of the distribution of power in the social structure. Important, if dated, essays on race and biology, preju-

dice and discrimination, class and power, marginality, institutional discrimination, ethnocentrism, racial conflict, desegregation, and protest movements. 468 pages.

Marable, Manning. *Blackwater: Historical Studies in Race, Class Consciousness, and Revolution.* Niwot: University Press of Colorado, 1993.
This collection of essays by an African American Marxist historian was first published in 1981. Includes essays on religion, resistance, and reactions to oppression. Marable provides a positive view of black nationalism. He describes revolutionary outbreaks of violence from Nat Turner to the Miami "rebellion" of May, 1980. 215 pages with an index.

Mason, Philip. *Patterns of Dominance.* London: Oxford University Press, 1970.
The author's masterful summary of race relations in South Africa, Brazil, the Caribbean, and the United States. Considers the conflict between whites and non-whites as a stage in human development, part of the collapse of colonialism and of the principle of inequality. We are faced with the terrible job of creating a society in which groups can live together and begin to recognize some degree of equality and justice for all. Before that is possible, nations must create minimum standards of wealth, power, esteem, and equality. Fear, greed, and jealousy stand in the way as does "the unruly self." These values are not easily overcome. 377 pages with a reading list, notes, and an index.

_____. *Prospero's Magic: Some Thoughts on Class and Race.* London: Oxford University Press, 1962.
A brief but brilliant discussion of race relations in England that is still significant for an understanding of American history. Based on the author's experiences as a diplomat and scholar in England, India, and the West Indies. Sees three main stages in race relations: first, a slave is a slave, but you can eat and talk with him because he is human. Second, after emancipation comes a period of challenge and rivalry. Here there is growing bitterness and hatred as the once dominant race becomes frightened and resentful because of its loss of status. Third is the crisis stage where the dominant group makes some concessions in terms of more equality and liberty but is greeted by refusal of anything except full human rights for the exploited class. This last cycle seems to have no end. 151 pages.

_____. *Race Relations.* New York: Oxford University Press, 1970.

A brilliant summary of the views of historians and anthropologists. Beliefs about race are important, race itself, however, is not. Discusses physical, psychological, and social causes of racism in South Africa and the United States. Modern urban life increases the significance of distinctions based on color. In the anonymity of cities, appearance becomes the only guide to social status and racial stereotypes are increasingly important. A common escape is withdrawal into a small world sealed against any contact with any group that is different. When the dam of segregation breaks, however, the results are usually catastrophic. 181 pages with a select bibliography and an index.

Masuoka, Jitsuichi, and Presten Valien, eds. *Race Relations: Problems and Theory, Essays in Honor of Robert E. Park.* Chapel Hill: University of North Carolina Press, 1971.
Thirteen essays written to honor the great sociologist at the University of Chicago who developed a new view of race relations in the 1920's. Contributors include E. Franklin Frazier, Everett Hughes, and other prominent sociologists of the 1940's and 1950's. Frazier's essay on "Racial Problems in World Society" (pages 38-51) is well worth reading. 290 pages with an index.

Montagu, M. F. Ashley. *Race: Man's Most Dangerous Myth.* New York: Columbia University Press, 1942. 5th rev. ed. New York: Oxford University Press, 1974. An old but still useful survey of misconceptions concerning the idea of race. Written in response to Nazi concepts of race by an eminent American anthropologist. 178 pages with a index.

_____, ed. *Race and I.Q.* New York: Oxford University Press, 1975.
A collection of essays attacking racial interpretations of intelligence. Montagu finds that environment and culture have far greater influences of the development of the mind than do genes or "racial inheritances." Includes an index.

Myrdal, Gunnar. *An American Dilemma: The Negro Problem and Modern Democracy.* 2 vols. New York: Harper & Row, 1944.
The classic study of race relations in the United States. An optimistic view asserting that white Americans will one day recognize the discrepancy between their belief in equality for all and the mistreatment handed out to blacks and other minorities. This support for the American Creed will win out in the end since Americans want to be rational and just. The gap between the ideal and the reality of segregation would end. Even the greatest fear of whites, interracial sex, would gradually disappear through education and contact. For a discussion of the great

significance of this work, see David W. Southern's *Gunnar Myrdal and Black-White Relations*, cited below. 1,535 pages with a bibliography, extensive notes, and an index.

Nash, Gary B., and Richard Weiss, eds. *The Great Fear: Race in the Mind of America*. New York: Holt, Rinehart and Winston, 1970.
Nine essays exploring white racial attitudes and their impact on American history from colonial times to the 1960's. Discussions of Native Americans, African Americans, Mexican Americans, and Asians. Nash's "Origins of Racism in Colonial America" is quite good. 214 pages with a bibliography and an index.

Nieman, Donald G. *Promises to Keep: African-Americans and the Constitutional Order, 1776 to Present*. New York: Oxford University Press, 1991.
A brief history of the relationship between African Americans and constitutional law. Discusses the influence of politics, ideology, and social forces in the development of civil rights legislation. Concludes that the promise of equality has not been achieved and that, instead, the law has served as a tool of white supremacy. We live in and have always lived in a segregated society. Principles such as states' rights and local control have functioned to promote and protect racial oppression. 275 pages with a bibliographical essay, a table of key civil rights cases, notes, and an index.

Parsons, Talcott. *Essays in Sociological Theory*. Glencoe, Ill.: The Free Press, 1954.
Contains the famed sociologist's "Revised Analytical Approach to Social Stratification," which describes the stratification theory of race relations. Race and ethnicity preserve independent social pyramids within the general social structure. Class lines are defined within these structures, upward mobility is difficult, and relations across pyramid and class lines are almost impossible. A much more rigid, inflexible, changeless system than the more free-flowing pluralist theory popular among many social scientists. In a pluralist system different sections of the community live side-by-side, have political representation, and achieve progress through upward mobility which is possible for all qualified people. Regrettably, Parsons does not have a lucid writing style.

Reimers, David M., ed. *Racism in the United States: An American Dilemma?* New York: Holt, Rinehart, 1972.

A brief collection of essays and documents in the "Problems in American Civilization" series. Surveys American attitudes from colonial times to the 1960's. 128 pages.

Rex, John. *Race Relations in Sociological Theory.* New York: Schocken Books, 1970.
A brief survey of important theories of racism, from Lloyd Warner in 1936 to Marvin Harris in the 1960's. Rex finds three elements common to all studies: There is inequality between groups, distinctions based on culture or ancestry, and justification of inequality based on a theory which need not be based on biology. Frequently it is based on religious or cultural differences. 169 pages with an index.

Rose, Peter I. *The Subject Is Race: Traditional Ideologies and the Teaching of Race Relations.* New York: Oxford University Press, 1968.
The results of a 1967 survey of 719 colleges concerning how they addressed courses on race relations. Describes the content of a variety of such courses and presents a survey of important historical and sociological literature that should be covered in the curriculum. 181 pages with a bibliography and an index.

Ruchames, Louis, ed. *Racial Thought in America: Vol. 1—From the Puritans to Abraham Lincoln.* Amherst: University of Massachusetts Press, 1969.
An excellent collection of original documents that provide a view of the development of racial thought from colonial times to the Civil War. Includes samples of pro- and anti-slavery thought, abolitionist pamphlets, freed slaves, and scientists of the time who defended slavery as legitimate in the Great Chain of Being. Each selection is ably introduced by the editor. 514 pages with an index.

Shipman, Pat. *The Evolution of Racism: Human Differences and the Use and Abuse of Science.* New York: Simon & Schuster, 1994.
A recent survey of scientific attitudes concerning the origins and significance of human races by a physical anthropologist. Pays particular attention to the views of Carlton Coon, Theodore Dobzhansky, and Ashley Montagu. Concludes that trying to define what constitutes a race is a futile exercise. An interesting discussion of genetics concluding that 90 percent of genes are common to all humans, while less than 1 percent differ significantly from each other. How can these differences be anything but trivial? Yet, they make huge differences in treatment and expectations of people of differing color in many places

throughout the world. 319 pages including a bibliography, notes, and an index.

Sigler, Jay A., ed. *International Handbook on Race and Race Relations.* Westport, Conn.: Greenwood Press, 1987.
Includes essays on almost every imaginable country that has racial problems. Also contains discussions and descriptions of North and South American, European, African, Indian, Asian, and Australian racial problems. Includes charts, notes, and an index. 483 pages.

Simpson, George E., and J. M. Yinger. *Racial and Cultural Minorities.* New York: Harper & Row, 1965.
A college level textbook discussing sociological and psychological theories of the causes and costs of racism. Includes a discussion of six policies by which a dominant group can treat a minority. Assimilation (forced and permitted), pluralism, legal protection for minorities, population transfer (peaceful or forced), continued subjugation, and extermination. Includes notes, a bibliography of social science literature, and an index.

Smith, J. Owens. *The Politics of Racial Inequality: A Systematic Comparative Macro-Analysis from the Colonial Period to 1970.* Westport, Conn.: Greenwood Press, 1987.
Results of an eight year study of why blacks have been unable to escape poverty, with a comparative view of Asians, Hispanics, and some European immigrant groups. Concludes that blacks have not received as much government assistance as did Europeans and other groups. Europeans received help, from the Homestead Act (1862), which gave them millions of acres of land, the National Labor Relations Act (1935), which enabled them to form unions (usually for whites only), and mortgage insurance programs. Because of racism on the part of white politicians blacks gained little from these programs and will continue to do poorly because of racial hatred and discrimination. A sobering view of the limitations of government programs and the racist nature of America's political system. 202 pages with a select bibliography, notes, and an index.

Sniderman, Paul M., and Thomas Piazza. *The Scar of Race.* Cambridge, Mass.: Harvard University Press, 1993.
A major compilation of surveys concerning racial attitudes in the United States as demonstrated in opinion polls conducted over forty years. Education is the one institution in American society that fights

the actual practice of racism more than any other. 212 pages with charts, graphs, and an index.

Southern, David W. *Gunnar Myrdal and Black-White Relations: The Use and Abuse of an American Dilemma, 1944-1969.* Baton Rouge: Louisiana State University Press, 1987.
Shows how Myrdal's great book and his ideas shaped the racial perceptions of a generation of social scientists, religious leaders, judges, and politicians. A useful summary of the values and ideas that helped bring and end to legal segregation and the positive influence of social scientists in changing attitudes toward race relations and inequality. For attitudes of social scientists before Myrdal, see the book by R. Fred Wacker cited below. 341 pages with extensive notes, a select bibliography, and an index.

Sowell, Thomas. *The Economics and Politics of Race: An International Perspective.* New York: William Morrow, 1983.
A black conservative economist surveys theories of race and genetic influences on intelligence. Returns to the idea that blacks were not enslaved because of theories of inferiority but simply because they became available as slaves at the right moment in time. Supports view that biology determines intelligence. Describes experience of Chinese, Europeans, and blacks in American society. 324 pages with notes and an index.

Stanfield, John H., II, ed. *A History of Race Relations Research: First Generation Recollections.* Newbury Park, Calif.: Sage Publications, 1993.
Interviews with major sociologists who have studied race relations. Includes discussions with Robert Blauner, Milton Gordon, Peter Rose, and Pierre L. Van den Berghe. These scholars talk about how and why they got into this field and offer their views of their contributions to the subject. 285 pages.

_____. *Philanthropy and Jim Crow in American Social Science.* Westport, Conn.: Greenwood Press, 1985
Presents case studies of pre-1945 social science research projects on race relations. Describes the development of financial support for the work of Robert E. Park and Gunnar Myrdal by foundations such as the Julius Rosenwald Fund and the Laura Spelman Rockefeller Foundation. Suggests that all studies were aimed at incorporating African Americans into a capitalist social order. 216 pages with tables, notes, and an index.

Stanton, William Ragan. *The Leopard's Spots: Scientific Attitudes Toward Race in America, 1815-59.* Chicago: University of Chicago Press, 1960.

A report on scientific explorations into the history of races and whether, as the debate was phrased at the time, the races sprang from one ancestor or many. Most experts concluded that the three races, Caucasian, Negroid, and Asiatic, were differently created. Africans were the weakest race and would die off very quickly outside of slavery. Being enslaved, then, was actually an advantage many early anthropologists argued. Americans who did not believe in scientific explanations—and that was the vast majority—simply accepted the biblical view, that slavery was ordained by God. 245 pages with extensive notes and an index.

Steinberg, Stephen. *The Ethnic Myth: Race, Ethnicity, and Class in America.* Boston: Beacon Press, 1989.

A book by a professor of urban studies that debunks the view that ethnicity is as important as race in American history. Race and class are the defining influences on people's lives, with race being used to prevent Americans, especially whites, from thinking in terms of social class. Also challenges the myth that race is declining in importance in American life. Racism is used to reinforce economic inequalities in American life and cannot be ignored when looking into the causes of poverty and crime. A challenging book that should be read by anyone interested in the problem of race relations. 317 pages with an index.

Stocking, George W., Jr. *Race, Culture and Evolution: Essays in the History of Anthropology.* New York: Free Press, 1968.

Treats aspects of early anthropological views of the significance of skin color in human life. An especially interesting chapter called "The Dark-Skinned Savage: The Image of Primitive Man in Evolutionary Anthropology" (pages 110-132). Savagery, as marked by dark skin, a small brain, and an incoherent mind, was still part of the African race, these students of human society believed. Civilization would have little influence on this creature, the scholars taught as late as the 1920's, who would maintain his dark skin and the incoherent mind of his race far into the future. 385 pages with notes and an index.

Takaki, Ronald T. *Iron Cages: Race and Culture in Nineteenth Century America.* New York: Alfred A. Knopf, 1979.

American race relations from the Revolution to the Spanish-American War of 1898. Focuses on the views of the culture-makers: politicians,

editors, novelists, educators, doctors, and businessmen. Includes discussions of Indians, Mexicans, and Asians, and how they were viewed
by the white majority. "Iron cages" was German sociologist Max
Weber's notion of how ideas trapped people in self-imposed confine-
ment. Whites were trapped by their racist views of superiority and did
significant damage to people they considered their inferiors. 361 pages
with notes and an index.

Van den Berghe, Pierre L. *Race and Racism: A Comparative Perspective.*
New York: John Wiley & Sons, 1967.
A brief but brilliant analysis of psychology and sociology of racism.
Describes two ideal types of multiracial societies: the paternalistic,
such as the slave-serf system, and the competitive or open system
where groups fight for status and wealth. In the first type, the dominant
group rules benevolently but treats the minority as inferior and unequal.
In the competitive system, class lines cut across race lines but ultimately race forms a stronger bond than social class. The working class
joins with the upper class to exclude and degrade the competing race.
Physical segregation takes place, contact between races declines, and
race hatred erupts into lynching and riots. 169 pages with an index.

Wacker, R. Fred. *Ethnicity, Pluralism, and Race: Race Relations Theory
in America Before Myrdal.* Westport, Conn.: Greenwood Press, 1983.
A very brief overview of sociological theories about race relations in
the 1920's and 1930's. Concentrates on the ideas to Robert E. Park and
the Chicago School of assimilationists who believed that blacks differed from European Americans in only minor ways. Conflict with
other groups was part of the process of moving into the American
mainstream. Prejudice and discrimination would eventually disappear
but only after a long period of fighting and competing for status and
wealth. 114 pages with a selected bibliography and an index.

Walvin, James. *Black and White: The Negro and English Society, 1555-
1945.* London: Penguin Press, 1973.
Images of blacks as seen by white English society. Whites responded
to blacks since earliest contacts with cruelty, indifference, and moral
insensitivity. A useful book because it demonstrates that racism and
racial violence is not limited to white American society. Color plays as
great a role in determining a person's position in British society as it
does in the United States. 239 pages with seventeen illustrations, a
bibliography, notes, and an index.

Wieviorka, Michel. *The Arena of Racism*. London: Sage Publications, 1995.

A brief book by a French sociologist discussing the spread of racism throughout the modern world. Racism unifies people and declaring others inferior beings creates a feeling of equality for the "superior" group. According to Wieviorka, racism has never gone away and never will. 148 pages with notes and an index.

Wilson, William Julius. *Power, Racism, and Privilege: Race Relations in Theoretical and Sociohistorical Perspectives*. New York: Macmillan, 1973.

A collection of essays on the emergence and development of racism in the United States. Economic and class differences cannot be understood without considering the long history of American prejudice and discrimination. Racism has long been used to justify the inferior and unequal treatment on black Americans. 224 pages with a bibliography and an index.

Woodward, C. Vann. *American Counterpoint: Slavery and Racism in the North-South Dialogue*. Boston: Little, Brown, 1971.

An important series of essays by a key historian of race relations in the United States. Ten essays concerning topics such as slavery in the Old South, the development of legal segregation, the emergence of white supremacy, and the development of the Civil Rights movement. Calls for a theory of race relations based on politics rather than economics, since politics brought about change, not industrialization or urbanization. The economic order of society conformed to the racial system. According to Woodward, racism existed in America whether in an agricultural, industrial, or urban economy. 301 pages with an index.

Zubaida, Sami, ed. *Race and Racialism*. London: Tavistock Publications, 1970.

Seven essays on race, racism, and race relations in the United States, South Africa, and South America by various experts. The essay by Michael Banton, "The Concept of Racism" (pages 17-33), summarizes the author's views briefly and intelligently. Generally race is seen as a political rather than a scientific concept. Equality is an ethical and political matter not subject to scientific verification. Racial determinism is seen as one of the great scientific errors of all time. 185 pages with references and an index.

Chapter 2

SLAVERY AND RACE IN NORTH AMERICA

GENERAL SURVEYS

Abzug, Robert H., and Stephen E. Maizlesh. *New Perspectives on Race and Slavery in America: Essays in Honor of Kenneth M. Stampp.* Lexington: University Press of Kentucky, 1986.
Ten essays collected in honor of the historian who wrote the first major post-World War II book on slavery. Essays on race and slavery, the psychology of race, Denmark Vesey's rebellion, African Americans in the Civil War, race relations in the period after the War, and a consideration of the views of the planter class. 206 pages with an index and brief notes. Most of the essays are excellent and contain useful summaries of key ideas about race relations in the South and North.

Blassingame, John W. *The Slave Community: Plantation Life in the Antebellum South.* Rev. ed. New York: Oxford University Press, 1979.
Originally published in 1972, Blassingame's work was the first study to view slavery from the point of view of slaves by incorporating plantation records, journals of slave owners, travelers' records, and autobiographies of slaves and free blacks. Blassingame concludes that there were many different types of slave personalities and that most maintained some remnants of African culture. Still a useful book for high school and college students because it says much about how slaves lived when they were beyond white control in the evenings and on weekends. An index, selected bibliography, and a essay on sources. 262 pages. For a critical view of this volume, see *Revisiting Blassingame's The Slave Community*, edited by Al-Tony Gilmore and cited below.

_____, ed. *Slave Testimony: Two Centuries of Letters, Speeches, Interviews, and Autobiographies.* Baton Rouge: Louisiana State University Press, 1977.
An interesting, huge collection of documents covering the period 1736 to 1878. Includes interviews, autobiographies, letters, speeches, and slave narratives collected in the 1920's and 1930's. There is a subject and name index. Twenty-five illustrations are included. Students will

find this a useful collection for doing research in original documents. 777 pages.

Boles, John B. *Black Southerners: 1619-1869.* Lexington: University Press of Kentucky, 1983.
A brief work discussing colonial slavery, industrial and urban slavery, the position of free blacks in southern society, and an especially interesting summary of slave religion. Racism emerged as the numbers of slaves grew and whites became concerned about maintaining unity and superiority. A well-written survey that students will guide students through changing attitudes toward African Americans and slavery. An index and bibliographical essay. 244 pages.

Bowser, Benjamin P., ed. *Racism and Anti-Racism in World Perspective.* Thousand Oaks, Calif.: Sage Publications, 1995.
Fifteen essays by specialists concerning racism in nations around the world. Peter H. Wood's "How the Myth of Race Took Hold and Flourished in the Mind's of Europe's Renaissance Colonizers" (pages 27-45) is especially interesting and informative about the origins of race-based slavery. 325 pages and an index.

David, Paul A., Herbert Gutman, Richard Sutch, Peter Temin, and Gavin Wright. *Reckoning with Slavery: A Critical Study in the Quantitative History of American Negro Slavery.* New York: Oxford University Press, 1976.
Written by five economic historians in response to Robert W. Fogel and Stanley Engerman's *Time on the Cross*, this work tries to expose the weaknesses and misleading statements found in that controversial work. Many charts and graphs and discussions of statistics. Written for the specialist, this book provides a page-by-page analysis of *Time on the Cross* and finds many errors of fact and interpretation. Includes an index, a bibliography, and a concordance to *Time on the Cross*. This 398-page work provides a useful example of how historians using the same evidence and "facts" can come up with widely differing interpretations.

Davis, David Brion. *The Problem of Slavery in Western Culture.* Ithaca, N.Y.: Cornell University Press, 1966.
The first in a classic three-volume survey of slavery in Western civilization, from ancient Greece and Rome to the 1770's. The discussion of the origins of the antislavery movement is especially interesting and innovative. Has an extensive bibliography of ancient texts, an index,

and detailed notes. 505 pages. Still useful as one of the few books that traces slavery back to its ancient roots.

_____. *The Problem of Slavery in the Age of Revolution, 1770-1823.* Ithaca, N.Y.: Cornell University Press, 1975.
Sees race as the central excuse for slavery and describes the rationale of slavery's defenders. Africans were savages and whites feared anarchy if they ever became free. Blacks had no discipline and would spend their time dancing, singing, gambling, and drinking. They would hang out in saloons, laugh at authority, and be unfit for work. Thus, they had to be kept unfree. Includes a discussion of abolitionist thought in Europe and the United States. This 576-page book contains an index and a splendid bibliography and is aimed at a scholarly audience.

_____. *Slavery and Human Progress.* New York: Oxford University Press, 1984.
A book aimed at scholars and a general audience which summarizes the author's extensive research and provides a view of slave systems from the ancient world to the twentieth century. The central conclusion: The abolitionist crusade against slavery emerged out of evangelical Protestantism and represented real progress in the world; evil can be fought against and defeated. There is no bibliography, but detailed notes and an index are provided.

Degler, Carl N. *Neither Black Nor White: Slavery and Race Relations in Brazil and the United States.* New York: Macmillan, 1971.
Prejudice against Africans preceded and led to enslavement. One answer to an old historical debate about which came first, race hatred or slavery? Africans were enslaved because they were available and already seen as weak, savage, and inferior. Brazil, however, never developed racial defense of slavery and escaped the ravages of North American racism after emancipation. Achieving full racial equality has proven much more difficult in the United States. Degler's book was among the first to compare slave systems in different countries. An excellent book by a leading historian. High school students and undergraduates can read this book.

Elkins, Stanley M. *Slavery: A Problem in American Institutional and Intellectual Life.* Chicago: University of Chicago Press, 1959.
A controversial work that compares slave life in America to the treatment of Jews in Nazi concentration camps. Slavery turned Africans into "Sambos" who were degraded, infantilized, and severely damaged psychologically, just as Jews were turned into childlike

creatures by the total brutality they experienced. Elkins' view has been challenged by many writers who believe his view exaggerated the harshness of treatment on plantations and downplayed the strength to survive found among slaves. Still worth reading for its depiction of slave life and its impact on the human mind. 264 pages with an index, extensive notes and brief list of sources.

Fogel, Robert W. *Without Consent or Contract: The Rise and Fall of American Slavery.* New York: W. W. Norton, 1989.
The author's revised views of conclusions reached in *Time on the Cross.* A discussion of the economics and conditions of slavery. Includes a comparison of antislavery movements in the United States and Europe. Slavery was very profitable but also maintained to control relations between blacks and whites. Includes an index and charts and tables illustrating everything from slave diets to the frequency of whippings. A massive amount of statistical evidence is included in two companion volumes, *Technical Papers: Markets and Production* and *Technical Papers: Conditions of Slaves Life and the Transition to Freedom* (1989), edited with economist Stanley Engerman. An additional supplement, subtitled *Evidence and Methods*, was published in 1992.

Fogel, Robert William, and Stanley L. Engerman. *Time on the Cross: The Economics of American Negro Slavery.* Boston: Little, Brown, 1974.
A controversial book that found slavery quite profitable for slave owners and almost benign for the slaves. Slavery taught Africans modern work habits of diligence, persistence, and efficiency. It was a progressive institution that brought slaves into contact with the modern world. Presents an idyllic view of slavery—slaves were well fed, housed, clothed, and doctored. They were much happier and contented than northern free laborers. A vast number of graphs, charts, and statistics are presented to prove this point. Engerman revises his view somewhat in *Without Consent or Contract.* See also *Reckoning with Slavery*, written by Paul A. David and four other economic historians and cited above.

Foner, Philip S. *History of Black Americans.* 3 vols. Westport, Conn.: Greenwood Press, 1975-1983.
A massive work by a recently deceased labor historian. Volume 1, which is 680 pages in length, begins with the African background of slavery and traces the history of slavery to the 1790's. Volume 2, which is 656 pages in length, raises issues of abolition, free blacks, and slave

revolts up to the 1850's. The final volume, which is 540 pages in length, carries African American history to the end of the Civil War. The set provides a detailed history with a Marxist perspective. Each volume has an index, bibliography, and many tables and charts. Useful for students interested in slave resistance and rebellions.

Franklin, John Hope. *Racial Equality in America.* Chicago: University of Chicago Press, 1976.
The author's 1976 Jefferson Lecture in Humanities delivered at the Library of Congress. A concise, expert view by the nation's most distinguished African American historian of slavery, segregation, discrimination and the social and economic costs of racism. A sobering view of race relations that finds that the end of slavery had no impact on the crusade for racial equality. Racism did not die, it became more degrading and destructive of hope and equality. 113 pages with suggestions for further reading. The author's views must be consulted by all students.

Franklin, John Hope, and Alfred A. Moss, Jr. *From Slavery to Freedom: A History of African Americans.* 7th ed. New York: McGraw-Hill, 1994.
The best single-volume history of African Americans. First published in 1947 this book has become a classic. It covers the entire history of Africans in the United States, the West Indies, and Latin America. Intended for use as a college text, it is filled with pictures, charts, maps, and excerpts from historical documents. Within its 680 pages, it includes a selected bibliography, an index, and appendixes containing key documents of the civil rights struggle. This book should be part of every American history course. It is well written, entertaining, and detailed.

Genovese, Eugene D. *In Red and Black: Marxian Explorations in Southern and Afro-American History.* New York: Pantheon Books, 1971.
Contains the author's essays and book reviews from 1965 to 1970 reflecting the political debates of the times, especially concerning questions of Black Power and black nationalism. Now dated but interesting simply to see the vigor with which such questions were discussed and argued. Also includes essays on socialism, black studies, and Marxism in America. Slavery severely damaged the black masses and they had yet to recover. 435 pages with an index and notes.

_____. *The Political Economy of Slavery: Studies in the Economy and Society of the Slave South.* 2d ed. Middletown, Conn.: Wesleyan University Press, 1989.

Originally published in 1961, this edition has a new introduction by the author discussing his changed views and judgments. The essays in the first edition are chiefly on economic aspects of the slave system covering such topics as productivity, subsistence, and slavery expansion. Genovese considers the slaveholders' point of view and finds them to be honorable and admirable men who represented a class that could only be changed by being crushed. This 336-page volume has an index and the original bibliographic note that is now dated.

_____. *Roll, Jordan, Roll: The World the Slaves Made.* New York: Pantheon Books, 1974.

An important interpretation by a leading historian of slavery. As with most Marxists, Genovese sees class rather than race as the key issue in the treatment of Africans and slaves. Whites had been enslaved in ancient times, and the master class had always hated and abused the lower class even when free and white. Blacks were not totally degraded under slavery. Instead, they created a separate black culture based on religion and communal suffering. 825 pages with a index and a long note on sources, including a list of key manuscript depositories. Genovese's landmark work deserves to be read by every student of race relations.

Gilmore, Al-Tony, ed. *Revisiting Blassingame's The Slave Community: The Scholars Respond.* Westport, Conn.: Greenwood Press, 1978.

Ten essays critical of Blassingame's view of slave culture and psychology. Historians such as Mary Frances Berry, George Rawick, Eugene Genovese, Stanley Engerman, and others criticize his methods of research. He leaves out female experience, for example, and neglects the more brutal aspects of master-slave relations. Blassingame responds to his critics in a lengthy essay. A useful volume for students to consult when reading *The Slave Community.* Includes an index and notes.

Greenberg, Kenneth S. *Masters and Statesmen: The Political Culture of American Slavery.* Baltimore: The Johns Hopkins University Press, 1985.

Describes the political values and practices of the slave society that emerged in the American South. What is the ideal master? According to Greenberg, it was a master who indicated that he was not possessed by a lust for power or motivated simply by greed. Respect came from his ability to prove his power and superiority by his kindness and generosity. Paradoxical, of course, but such were the expectations. 195 pages with an index.

Handlin, Oscar, and Mary Handlin. "Origins of the Southern Labor System." *William and Mary Quarterly* 3d ser., 7 (April, 1950): 199-222.
A key article leading to a long debate over the reasons behind enslave-ment of Africans. Argues that the first blacks in Jamestown (1619) lived as indentured servants, suffering little discrimination or mistreatment simply because they were black. Race hatred emerged only after the legalization of slavery in the 1660's. Africans were not hated because they were black but because they allowed themselves to become slaves. Hence, once they became free laborers again racial hatred would diminish.

Huggins, Nathan I. *Black Odyssey: The Afro-American Ordeal in Slavery.* New York: Pantheon Books, 1977.
An African American historian tries to capture the degradation and the desperation of the slave condition. He wants to make the reader feel the pain and agony and sometimes achieves poetry in his writing. This is the story of the triumph of the human spirit over great adversity. It is a narrative history told through songs, poems, and eyewitness accounts. There is a brief bibliographical note. An excellent book for a student with little knowledge of the subject.

Jordan, Winthrop D., ed. *The Negro Versus Equality, 1762-1826.* Chicago: Rand McNally, 1969.
Part of the Berkeley Series in American History, this brief collection (59 pages) of primary documents, introduced by the editor, containing the views of Americans such as James Otis, Thomas Jefferson, and Benjamin Rush on Africans, their history, nature, and future. The origins of race prejudice are found in the Garden of Eden (especially human nature), according to Jordan, and therefore are quite difficult to change. For a fuller discussion, see Jordan's *White Over Black*, cited below.

_____. *The White Man's Burden: Historical Origins of Racism in the United States.* New York: Oxford University Press, 1974.
An abridgment of *White Over Black* that contains the essentials of Jordan's argument, providing an overview of opinions ranging from medieval European views of blackness and Africans to the 1820's.

Includes an index and suggestions for further reading. Brief enough for high school students and undergraduates.

_____. *White Over Black: American Attitudes Toward the Negro, 1550-1812.* Chapel Hill: University of North Carolina Press, 1968.
Why were Africans enslaved? Because they were black—the color of darkness and dirt. Hatred of Africans and racial prejudice preceded slavery. Africans were savages who had to be controlled because of the psychological needs of whites. Blacks represented the worst instincts of humankind: lust, avarice, licentiousness, laziness, and other deadly sins, Europeans believed. If they were not controlled through by force white women would be raped and the white race and its purity would be greatly imperiled. A dark, brooding book that sees little hope for improved race relations. Includes a massive bibliography of medieval and modern sources, an index, and an essay on sources. 651 pages aimed at scholars and experts. For a useful summary of the author's views, see *The White Man's Burden*, cited above.

Klein, Herbert S. *Slavery in the Americas: A Comparative Study of Virginia and Cuba.* Chicago: University of Chicago Press, 1967. Reprint. Chicago: Ivan Dee, 1987.
A comparative study by a professor of Latin American history. Race was far more a factor in determining slavery in Virginia than in Cuba. Cuban slavery was based on the need for labor. Once Cuban landowners found slavery was unprofitable, they moved to free labor. Freedom in Virginia was much harder to attain; slavery could not be eradicated without a war because of the entrenched racial hatred of the ruling race. 270 pages with an index. Useful for students seeking to understand the background of race prejudice in the United States.

Kolchin, Peter. *American Slavery: 1619-1877.* New York: Hill & Wang, 1993.
A brief, informative survey of the history of slavery from 1619 to 1877. Slavery was a system of labor but it also kept blacks in a inferior position and maintained white supremacy. Color made slaves more visible and distinct, so slaves were more easily controlled and found. Whites saw Africans as unequal in intelligence and morally degraded, thus justifying the unequal treatment Africans received. The idea grew that ending slavery would endanger white freedom. In 304 pages the author presents a powerful argument and a sensitive portrayal of the slave condition. There is a excellent, detailed bibliography and an

index. All students can read this excellent summary of the history of slavery.

_____. *Unfree Labor: American Slavery and Russian Serfdom.* Cambridge, Mass.: Harvard University Press, 1987.
A comparative history of slavery in the United States and serfdom in Russia. Both systems of unfree labor supported wealthy landholders, serfdom being just another form of slavery. Southern whites and Russian aristocrats used similar defenses for their labor systems, they believed they were protecting their society from a class or race contaminated by decadence, greed, and filth. American slaves were better off materially than the Russian serfs. Slaveholders' self-interest demanded that slaves be fed and clothed so they could work harder. Landlords in Russia had no such motivation. Slaves and free blacks were outsiders in the South who could never, because of their color, be part of the political system. This 517-page book contains a bibliographical note, and index, and extensive notes. A unique cross-cultural view of slavery and inequality.

Lauber, Almon Wheeler. *Indian Slavery in Colonial Times Within the Present Limits of the United States.* 1913. Reprint. Williamstown, Mass.: Corner House, 1979.
Still the standard book on white attempts to enslave Native Americans. Includes discussion of Spanish, French, and English efforts to enslave, all of which failed. Discusses legislation, regulation, and treatment in all colonies. 352 pages with an index.

Levine, Lawrence. *Black Culture and Black Consciousness: Afro-American Thought from Slavery to Freedom.* New York: Oxford University Press, 1977.
A unique work that offers an intellectual history of slaves and their reactions to freedom. Slave thinking is captured through a discussion of songs, folktales, jokes, oral poetry, folk songs, popular songs, hymns, and the blues. The author, a historian, has written a wonderful book that captures the spirit of a people and sensitively describes their thoughts, feelings, and dreams. 522 pages with an index and many notes. Useful and informative for any teacher, student, or interested reader.

McManus, Edgar J. *Black Bondage in the North.* Syracuse, N.Y.: Syracuse University Press, 1973.
Racial attitudes in the northern colonies were the key to maintaining slavery until the American Revolution. White dominance was based on

a feeling of superiority which was not mitigated by religion or law. From 1619 to the 1780's, there is little evidence that northern whites felt any differently toward slaves than did their counterparts in the South. 236 pages with an index and a bibliographical essay.

Meier, August, and Elliott Rudwick. *Black History and the Historical Profession, 1915-1980.* Urbana: University of Illinois Press, 1986.
From Carter Woodson to Eugene Genovese and others, this collection of five essays reveals the concerns of historians, their lives, motives, and interests. Based on dozens of interviews conducted by two leading historians of the African American experience, the book focuses on historians of the black experience, their points of view, and how they came to be interested in African American history. 382 pages with an index and notes.

_____. *From Plantation to Ghetto: An Interpretive History of American Negroes.* 3d ed. New York: Hill & Wang, 1976.
From the African background to the Civil Rights revolution, this work provides a brief history of ideologies, protest movements, race riots, and white violence. Includes sections on slavery in the cities, blacks in the Civil War, lynching, and the origins of the modern civil rights crusade. 406 pages with a selected bibliography and an index.

_____, eds. *The Making of Black America.* Vol. 1: *Origins of Black Americans*; Vol. 2: *The Black Community in Modern America.* New York: Atheneum, 1969-1976.
Essays by sociologists, historians, political scientists, and historians on race relations, economics, demography, and ideology. The first volume begins with the African background, and includes key essays on slave law, free blacks in the South, the Civil War, and Reconstruction. Volume 2 has discussions of the origins of segregation, Booker T. Washington, the Populist Party and blacks, the Ku Klux Klan, the modern Civil Rights movement, school desegregation, and Martin Luther King, Jr. 389 pages and 507 pages.

Mellon, James, ed. *Bullwhip Days: The Slaves Remember.* New York: Weidenfeld & Nicolson, 1988.
A collection of twenty-nine slave narratives from the Federal Writers' Project of the Works Progress Administration (WPA). Surviving slaves tell of the cruelty and brutality of slavery and its aftermath. Many photographs and pictures of former slaves, their families, and their homes. A great place to start for students in high school or college. 460 pages. No index or bibliography. All of the narratives (more than two

thousand) are in the series *The American Slave: A Composite Autobiography*, edited by George P. Rawick and cited below.

Meltzer, Milton, ed. *The Black Americans: A History in Their Own Words.* New York: Harper & Row, 1984.
A collection of documents with introductions by the author. It includes "Nat Turner's Confession," and "Daniel Walker's Appeal to the Colored Citizens of the World," newspaper accounts of lynchings, Ku Klux Klan pamphlets, and statements by Booker T. Washington and W. E. B. Du Bois. For high school students. The final section includes excerpts from the trial of the Scottsboro boys, Harlem Renaissance poetry and literature, and publications of the Civil Rights movement. Individual introductions to the documents help place them in their appropriate contexts.

Moore, Wilbert E. *American Negro Slavery and Abolition: A Sociological Study.* New York: Third Press, 1971. Reprint. New York: Arno Press, 1980.
Written by a sociologist, this volume finds that religion was as important as race in the defense of slavery. Africans were "heathenish" and therefore could be enslaved. Ideas of inherent racial inferiority developed after enslavement as an added justification. A brief work (199 pages), with notes and an index. It adds little new to the debate over slavery's origins or its demise.

Morgan, Edmund. *American Slavery, American Freedom.* New York: W. W. Norton, 1975.
A major work by an eminent American historian that finds race prejudice at the heart of American slavery. Would slave masters have treated whites so harshly? Definitely not, the author concludes. Race prejudice and slavery were introduced into Virginia by white landlords interested in keeping poor whites and blacks from joining together in common cause against their masters. Bacon's Rebellion of 1676, which almost overthrew the ruling class, showed the power of whites who suffered economic distress. Slavery of blacks provided total social control and would keep Africans from making common cause with poor whites in any future rebellions. 454 pages with an index, a note on sources, extensive notes, and a few illustrations.

Mullin, Michael. *American Negro Slavery: A Documentary History.* Columbia: University of South Carolina Press, 1976.
An unusual yet helpful collection of records from colonial times to the Civil War. Excerpts from owner's diaries, plantation account books,

newspaper advertisements for runaway slaves, church records, deeds and wills, court records and legal codes. The documents concentrate on describing the everyday lives of slaves on plantations and off. Extremely well edited and introduced. Includes an index, 288 pages.

Owens, Harry P., ed. *Perspectives and Irony in American Slavery.* Jackson: University Press of Mississippi, 1976.
Six essays by major scholars given at a bicentennial conference sponsored by the University of Mississippi. David Brion Davis, Eugene Genovese, Carl Degler, Stanley Engerman, John Blassingame, and Kenneth Stampp present brief essays summarizing their views and defending their positions. Stampp has a particularly interesting bibliographic essay responding to criticism of his work. 188 pages with a brief list of sources, no index.

Owens, Leslie Howard. *This Species of Property: Slave Life and Culture in the Old South.* New York: Oxford University Press, 1976.
A discussion of how slaves lived with sections on disease, medical care, labor, diet. work in the household and the field, slave drivers, folklore, music, religion, magic, and l'fe. A successful attempt to portray slaves' experiences and present a sense of their existence. 291 pages with an index, notes, and an extensive list of manuscript sources. Most high school students and undergraduates would find this work extremely useful in understanding the way slaves lived.

Parish, Peter J. *Slavery: History and the Historians.* New York: Harper & Row, 1989.
A British historian reviews the major historical works on slavery and offers his criticism. A useful place to begin research on slavery in the United States. Has a brief summary of all the major issues and asks valuable questions about what is still needed in slavery research. 224 pages with an index.

Patterson, Orlando. *Slavery and Social Death: A Comparative Study.* Cambridge, Mass.: Harvard University Press, 1982.
Discusses and compares slavery in sixty-six societies, including the United States, Brazil, and Cuba. Explores the history of slavery to its origins in Mesopotamia. Slavery was based on race in many societies including the ancient ones. It grew more important, however, in the New World and slavery was a result only of race here. Slavery was a relationship based on human parasitism that destroyed millions of lives in defense of racial superiority. The author is a sociologist and leading student of race relations. 511 pages, three maps, and several appendices

comparing slavery and treatment of slaves around the world. An index and extensive notes.

Quarles, Benjamin. *The Negro in the Making of America.* 3d ed. New York: Collier Books, 1987.
Originally published in 1964 by a distinguished African American historian who shows deep compassion for his people, this is an excellent one-volume history extending from 1619 to the 1980's. At 362 pages, it is brief enough to be used as a supplement in a history survey class. Discusses African Americans in the process of assimilation and transformation of American culture. The third edition includes a revised bibliography, as well as an index and notes.

Rawick, George P., ed. *The American Slave: A Composite Autobiography.* 18 vols. Westport, Conn.: Greenwood Press, 1972.
Contain the previously unpublished interviews of former slaves conducted in the 1930's by writers with the Works Progress Administration. Former slaves discuss their lives, folklore, poetry, and music. Narratives from South Carolina, Texas, Alabama, Indiana, Oklahoma, Mississippi, Arkansas, Missouri, Georgia, North Carolina, and Florida are included in that order. Most of the material concerns conditions after 1835, no one was alive from before then, and most of the former slaves interviewed were in their eighties and nineties. The collection includes two volumes of interviews collected by Fisk University scholars in the 1920's. After reading only a few of these reminiscences, one becomes overwhelmed by the brutality of slavery and racism and the courage of the survivors. An index to the collection is provided by Donald M. Jacobs' *Index to the American Slave*, published by Greenwood Press in 1989.

_____. *From Sundown to Sunup: The Making of the Black Community.* Vol. 1 in *The American Slave: A Composite Autobiography.* Westport, Conn.: Greenwood Press, 1972.
The introductory volume to an eighteen-book collection of slave narratives collected in the 1930's by the Works Progress Administration (WPA). Rawick, a sociologist, portrays life in the slave quarters and discusses the attitudes that kept Africans enslaved. Whites, from the most reactionary and brutal to the most humane and paternalistic, shared the view that whites and blacks could never meet on an equal level. Freedom and equality meant interracial marriage, whites were convinced, and that was the worst thing possible because it would lead to utter degradation of "the master race." Slavery had to be maintained

so blacks could be controlled and kept in their place. 166 pages with notes, and index, and a brief bibliography.

Rose, Willie Lee. *A Documentary History of Slavery in North America.* New York: Oxford University Press, 1976.
Documents from Jamestown in 1619 to the conclusion of the Civil War in 1865. Letters, laws, diaries, records of insurrections from local newspapers, advertisement for slave auctions and sales, state slave codes, court decisions challenging mistreatment of slaves, folktales, memoirs, wills, games, riddles, hymns, and songs. This 537-page work is probably the best single-volume collection of documents, each skillfully edited and introduced. Includes an introduction to sources and an index.

————. *Slavery and Freedom.* Edited by William W. Freehling. New York: Oxford University Press, 1982.
The collected essays and book reviews of a prominent historian of slavery who suffered a stroke and was unable to complete her work. The editor has collected her major essays in this volume. Slavery changed over time and grew more benevolent after 1800 until 1840 when there was a reversion to mistreatment. Even as slave owners became kinder, freedom became more difficult to obtain and slaves grew more dependent on their masters. Essays on John Brown, free blacks, and the impact of the American Revolution are included. 224 pages with a index and a short bibliographic note.

Singleton, Theresa A. *The Archaeology of Slavery and Plantation Life.* Orlando, Fla.: Academic Press, 1985.
A unusual collection of fourteen essays by anthropologists and archaeologists concerning slave culture, including housing styles, food and cooking, and family and social structure. Pictures, graphs, charts, and maps are used to draw a detailed view of everyday slave life. 338 pages including a bibliography of anthropological works about slavery, an index, and a statistical appendix.

Stampp, Kenneth M. *The Peculiar Institution: Slavery in the Antebellum South.* New York: Alfred A. Knopf, 1956.
The first work that challenged traditional views of slavery developed by U. B. Phillips in the early twentieth century. Phillips argued that slavery was beneficial to blacks because it brought them into civilization. It was also unprofitable for whites. Stampp assumes that African Americans were "only white men with black skins," a radical view even for its times. Slavery was not purely an economic institution but

it was a part of a social pattern that lived on after emancipation. Slavery was a system of regulating human beings considered to be dangerous, savage, and lazy and after the Civil War it was replaced by segregation. 436 pages with an index, detailed notes, and a bibliography that cites many pre-1945 works on the slave question.

Tannenbaum, Frank. *Slave and Citizen: The Negro in the Americas.* New York: Random House, 1946.
A study of race relations and slavery in North and South America. Suggests that slavery in North America was less harsh and violent than in South America. Although the thesis of this classic work has been shown to be incorrect, the paternalistic brand of slavery found in North America probably was less savage than the Brazilian or Cuban systems.

Thomas, Laurence Mordekhai. *Vessels of Evil: American Slavery and the Holocaust.* Philadelphia: Temple University Press, 1993.
An unusual work by an philosopher that compares the horrors suffered by African Americans and Jews. 211 pages of speculation and conclusions about the consequences of racism. Raises many interesting questions but pays little attention to modern views of slavery. An index but no bibliography.

Van DeBurg, William L. *Slavery and Race in American Popular Culture.* Madison: University of Wisconsin Press, 1984.
An interesting, brief, work that describes how novelists, historians, dramatists, poets, filmmakers, songwriters, and television have looked at and interpreted the experience of slaves. Covers material from the 1600's to contemporary times. The view of slavery, the author concludes, explains much about white anxieties and the African American desire for equality. 263 pages with notes, a selected bibliography, and an index. Unusual and well worth reading.

Walker, Clarence E. *Deromanticizing Black History: Critical Essays and Reappraisals.* Knoxville: University of Tennessee Press, 1991.
A book of challenging essays by a African American historian who calls for a more believable, less romanticized portrait of black culture and life. History should pay attention so the strengths and weaknesses of black people in bondage. The social and psychological tensions of being enslaved must be more realistically portrayed. According to Walker, historians have painted too rosy a picture of conditions of life in slave quarters and ghettoes. Writers have ignored the self-abuse, self-hatred, and color prejudice within the black community. A call for history that goes beyond the notion that oppression produced only kind

and generous heroes. The same standards of criticism should be applied to "the people" that are used to judge the elite. 164 pages with a brief bibliography, index, and notes. An interesting counterpoint to traditional views of African American history.

Weinstein, Allen, Frank Otto Gattell, and David Sarasohn. *American Negro Slavery: A Modern Reader.* New York: Oxford University Press, 1978.

Contains fourteen key essays on slavery and slave culture. Includes the views of George Frederickson on race relations and slavery, as well as David Brion Davis, Robert W. Fogel and Stanley Engerman, Herbert Gutman on African American families, Eugene Genovese, Stanley Elkins, and others. The best single-volume collection of modern interpretations of slavery. 317 pages with an index and bibliography.

Chapter 3

SLAVERY AND RACE

Abrahams, Roger D. *Singing the Master: The Emergence of African American Culture in the Plantation South.* New York: Pantheon Books, 1992.
A study of the annual plantation corn-shucking celebration and the harvest and festival that surrounded it, written by a professor of folklore and folklife. To the white masters, the event was entertainment and kept slaves happy and contented. For the slaves, however, the eating and dancing helped perpetuate African culture and encouraged mutual participation and community development. 341 pages with an index. Interesting reading that provides a detailed examination of how one African ceremony survived the slave experience.

Alford, Terry. *Prince Among Slaves.* New York: Harcourt Brace Jovanovich, 1977.
The biography of an African prince captured in 1788 at the age of twenty-six and taken to a plantation in Natchez, Mississippi, where he worked for forty years. As a slave, he maintained a strict code of discipline and kept his self-respect. After being freed by his master, he returned to his African homeland to die. This well-written volume demonstrates how slaves could even under the harshest conditions maintain a sense of dignity and worthiness. There is an extensive genealogy and detailed notes. Highly recommended for general American history survey courses.

Barr, Alwyn. *Black Texans: A History of African Americans in Texas, 1528-1995.* Norman: University of Oklahoma Press, 1996.
Originally published in 1973, this is one of the few books that traces the history of African Americans in a single state from the earliest times to recent events. Describes Spanish attitudes toward slavery and race and has a lengthy discussion of segregation and white supremacy in the aftermath of the Civil War. Includes a bibliography and an index.

Bateman, Fred, and Thomas Weiss. *A Deplorable Scarcity: The Failure of Industrialization in the Slave Economy.* Chapel Hill: University of North Carolina Press, 1981.
A statistical analysis of why slavery did not seem to work in cities and industrial establishments. Concludes that white fear of slave rebellions was a major reason for the failure of the slave system in these areas. 237 pages with tables, census data, and an index.

Berlin, Ira, and Ronald Hoffman, eds. *Slavery and Freedom in the Age of the American Revolution.* Charlottesville: University Press of Virginia, 1983.
Nine essays by prominent historians presented at the United States Historical Society's 1979 symposium. The essays cover the period from 1775 to 1783 and discuss the African American experience in northern cities, the Loyalist army, the South, and the migration by some to the Caribbean. 341 pages with an index.

Boles, John B., ed. *Masters and Slaves in the House of the Lord: Race and Religion in the American South, 1740-1870.* Lexington: University Press of Kentucky, 1981.
Nine essays that probe black participation in white churches and the white mission to convert slaves to Christianity. Nothing specifically on African American religion, but scholarly essays on "Biracial Fellowship," "Catholicism and Slavery," and the origin of African American churches in the aftermath of emancipation. 257 pages with an index and notes.

Boskin, Joseph. *Into Slavery: Racial Decisions in the Virginia Colony.* Washington, D.C.: University Press of America, 1979.
A study of the controversial question of when slavery actually began in the English colonies. Concludes slavery emerged in Virginia in the 1660's with laws providing for lifelong servitude. Slavery was based on race alone and a child inherited the condition of his or her mother. Interracial marriage was strictly forbidden. Includes twenty-five original documents from legal codes and court records. A brief 115-page summary of the problem with an index and bibliographic guide to early court records.

Breen, T. H., and Stephen Innes. *"Myne Owne Ground": Race and Freedom on Virginia's Western Shore, 1640-1676.* New York: Oxford University Press, 1980.
English colonists and Africans interacted with one another as relative equals for two generations from the 1640's to the 1670's. Concludes

that slavery was not legally mandated until passage of a slave code after Bacon's Rebellion, which involved white former indentured servants, in 1676. This 142-page volume explains the story of free blacks in one Virginia county who owned their own land and moved about without constraint. Then slavery and prejudice reduced the free population to insecurity and thievery. It was not simply racial prejudice but the need for a stable labor force that produced slavery.

Campbell, Randolph B. *An Empire for Slavery: The Peculiar Institution in Texas, 1821-1865*. Baton Rouge: Louisiana State University Press, 1989.
A survey of the economic and legal foundations of slavery from the time of the Mexican Revolution to the end of the Civil War. Based on slave narratives collected by the Works Progress Administration (WPA) in the 1930's, this work discusses the physical and psychological effects of slavery on the African American population and their white masters. Campbell sees the greed of the planters as the major cause of slavery. 306 pages with an index and an extensive bibliography. Includes many tables and statistics that are easy to understand.

Cooper, William J., Jr. *Liberty and Slavery: Southern Politics to 1860*. New York: Alfred A. Knopf, 1983.
A history of white politicians and how they used the issue of slavery to promote white solidarity. The liberty to own slaves was the key to freedom for all whites in the South. Enslaving Africans ensured the progress of civilization and the unity of the white race. 310 pages with an index, notes, and a brief bibliographical essay.

_____. *The South and the Politics of Slavery, 1828-1856*. Baton Rouge: Louisiana State University Press, 1978.
A general survey of the defense of slavery and even occasional opposition to it in state legislatures and elections. Includes notes and an index.

Cope, Robert S. *Carry Me Back: Slavery and Servitude in Seventeenth Century Virginia*. Pikeville, Ky.: Pikeville College Press, 1973.
Although it is difficult to find, this work contains a useful description and comparison of indentured servitude and the enslavement of Africans between 1619 and 1680. Cope answers the question of why slavery became the lot for most blacks. The large turnover of indentured servants, who served for about five years, made the workforce unstable and free laborers charged exorbitant wages, at least in the eyes of the plantation owners. Slavery provided extremely cheap labor, and

Africans were adopted already to the hot humid climate. As a result, slavery appeared to be more economical and practical than indentured servitude. 179 pages with an index and a bibliography.

Craven, Wesley Frank. *White, Red, and Black: The Seventeenth-Century Virginian.* Charlottesville: University Press of Virginia, 1971. Reprint. New York: W. W. Norton, 1977.
An attempt to tell the story of English, African, and Native American interactions in colonial Virginia. A multicultural approach that describes the influences of each culture on the other. Also portrays the deep feelings of racial hatred that divided peoples in the 1600's. Has notes, a bibliography, and an index.

Davis, Charles T., and Henry Louis Gates, Jr., eds. *The Slave's Narrative.* New York: Oxford University Press, 1985.
A collection of essays and documents concerning the history, nature, and function of slave autobiographies and narratives from 1750 to modern times. Analysis by literary critics and historians. Excerpts from dozens of original works by slaves and former slaves and a useful introduction on "The Language of Slavery" by the two editors, both distinguished literary critics. 342 pages with an index and an extensive bibliography listing most important slave narrative.

Davis, Edwin Adams, and William Ransom Hogan, eds. *The Barber of Natchez.* Baton Rouge: Louisiana State University Press, 1973.
Excerpts from the two-thousand-page diary of William Johnson, a freed slave in Mississippi who operated and owned several barber shops and other businesses from 1835 to 1851. Johnson speaks of the prejudice and discrimination he faced. His life ended tragically when he was murdered by a white man in a dispute over property ownership. Originally published as *William Johnson's Natchez: The Antebellum Diary of a Free Negro* (1951). 272 pages. No index.

Deetz, James. *Flowerdew Hundred: The Archaeology of a Virginia Plantation, 1619-1864.* Charlottesville: University Press of Virginia, 1993.
The results of more than twenty-five years of excavations of house foundations, fortifications, wells, and trash pits. Deetz's study includes twenty-three photographs of material objects used by slaves and masters in their kitchens and fields as well as thirty-four drawings and illustrations of architecture, farm implements, and cooking utensils. According to Deetz, the archaelogical evidence from the Flowerdew site suggests a gradual decline in standards for slave diet and housing.

204 pages with an index, notes, and select bibliography of other archaeological studies of slave culture.

Fehrenbacher, Don E. *The Dred Scott Case: Its Significance in American Law and Politics.* New York: Oxford University Press, 1978.
The masterwork on the most important legal case involving slavery. Not just a legal history, however, but a detailed discussion of the legal history of slavery back to its earliest days and a sympathetic portrait of the individuals involved in this case. Slaves were declared noncitizens and non-humans by the United States Supreme Court here and Fehrenbacher explains why. An index and a bibliography.

Fields, Barbara Jeanne. *Slavery and Freedom on the Middle Ground: Maryland During the Nineteenth Century.* New Haven, Conn.: Yale University Press, 1985.
Generally covers the time period from 1850 to 1877. Fields discusses the end of slavery and the difficult transition to freedom and explores how slaves and their masters sought to restore some understanding of each other after the death of slavery. Based on Freedmen's Bureau records and documents, Fields's work contains extensive quotes from both races concerning their view of slavery and its end. Unfortunately, the book is marred by occasional lapses in clarity. Includes seventeen tables and charts describing economic and social conditions, a map, extensive notes, and an index.

Finkelman, Paul, ed. *The Law of Freedom and Bondage: A Case Book.* New York: Oceana Publications, 1986.
A series of judicial decisions, introduced by the editor, that discuss the criminal law of slavery from its origins through the debate over manumission and abolition. The last case dates to 1864. A 281-page work with an index.

_____. *Slavery and the Founders: Race and Liberty in the Age of Jefferson.* Armonk, N.Y.: M. E. Sharpe, 1996.
Explores how the first generation of political leaders, from George Washington to James Madison, dealt with the issue of slavery. Thomas Jefferson's views are described in great detail. 228 pages with notes and an index.

_____, ed. *Slavery, Race, and the American Legal System, 1700-1872.* 16 vols. New York: Garland, 1988.
A massive collection of facsimile reproductions containing more than one hundred and seventy rare pamphlets. The series includes *Southern*

Slaves in Free Courts (3 vols.), *Abolitionists in Northern Courts, The African American Slave Trade and American Courts* (2 vols.), *Fugitive Slaves and American Courts* (4 vols.), *Slave Rebels, Abolitionists, and Southern Courts* (2 vols.), *Free Blacks, Slaves, and Slave Owners in Civil and Criminal Courts* (2 vols.), *Free Blacks, Slaves, and Slave Owners in Civil and Criminal Courts* (2 vols.), and *Statutes on Slavery* (2 vols.). Many of the pamphlets are difficult to read in their facsimile form but there is certainly very little missing here for those interested in comments on court cases and other judicial decisions. Each pamphlet includes a brief introduction by the series editor.

Freehling, Alison Goodyear. *Drift Toward Dissolution: The Virginia Slavery Debate of 1831-32.* Baton Rouge: Louisiana State University Press, 1982.
A discussion of the debate over whether to ban slavery in Virginia which took place in the legislature after the Nat Turner rebellion in 1831. The debate showed a severely divided white community fearful of continuing rebellions. Fifty-five whites had been killed by Nat Turner's supporters and some legislators thought only immediate emancipation would prevent future bloodshed. That idea was rejected, however, as tighter control of the slave population seemed to offer a better method of preventing rebellions. A well-written book with an index, bibliography, five maps, several illustrations, and a few tables.

Fry, Gladys-Marie. *Night Riders in Black Folk History.* Knoxville: University of Tennessee Press, 1975.
Based on oral history, an interesting study of the psychological damage caused by fear and terror. Studies the methods used by whites to control the African American population in the aftermath of the Civil War. Fear of ghosts and the supernatural was used by whites to discourage black mobility. The Ku Klux Klan and "night riders" created a culture of fear which had its roots in African beliefs in witches, the walking dead, and deceased ancestors. Fry uses WPA and Fisk University interviews from the 1930's to find evidence of extreme fear of white terrorist groups. 251 pages with a few illustrations, a brief bibliography, and an index.

Gara, Larry. *The Liberty Line: The Legend of the Underground Railroad.* Lexington: University Press of Kentucky, 1961.
Finds the number of "passengers" on the Underground Railroad to be greatly exaggerated with the legend being far more important than the reality. No more than three thousand slaves escaped to the North every

year out of a population that by 1860 reached almost four million. 201 pages with an index.

Goldin, Dale. *Urban Slavery in the American South, 1820-1860: A Quantitative History.* Chicago: University of Chicago Press, 1976.
Goldin challenges the widely held belief set forth by Richard Wade that cities and slavery were not compatible. Demand for slaves was quite strong in southern cities, and there were no inherent forces in the structures or urban life, such as closer contact with free blacks and whites, that caused the system to decline in urban areas. 168 pages with thirty-four tables, an index, extensive notes and a bibliography. Some of the statistics make for heavy going while reading, but this is an important criticism of the traditional view of slavery in cities.

Hall, Gwendolyn M. *Africans in Colonial Louisiana: The Development of Afro-Creole Culture in the Eighteenth Century.* Baton Rouge: Louisiana State University Press, 1992.
A survey of race relations in French colonial Louisiana that traces conflict between red, white, and black populations. The racial heritage of colonial Louisiana was one of violence, corruption, and brutal hatred. The author traces the history of a slave uprising in 1795 that saw twenty-three slaves hung and then decapitated after an alleged conspiracy was broken. Racial terror increased against blacks throughout the colony in the aftermath. A thoroughly researched and well-written book that uses many French colonial sources demonstrating that racism was a peculiarly British attitude. 434 pages with maps, nineteen charts, fourteen tables, a brief note on sources, and an index.

Higginbotham, A. Leon, Jr. *In the Matter of Color: The Colonial Period.* New York: Oxford University Press, 1978.
A study of laws throughout the colonies, from 1619 to 1787, which shows how the law itself created a spirit of racial repression. The law was used as an instrument to protect injustice and inequality. Part of the Race and the American Legal Process series, this survey by a African American lawyer and federal judge demonstrates that colonial law was never color-blind. 512 pages with a bibliography, a table of important cases, and an index.

Hoffer, Peter Charles, ed. *Africans Become Afro-Americans: Selected Articles on Slavery in the American Colonies.* New York: Garland, 1988.
Contains eighteen important essays by key scholars in the field including, Oscar Handlin, Stanley Elkins, Carl Degler, Winthrop Jordan,

Stanley Engerman, Edward Morgan, Peter Wood, Allan Kulikoff, and Ira Berlin. The only collection with all the key articles on slavery, since 1957, each ably introduced by the editor. 442 pages. Part of the eighteen-volume *Essays in Early American History: A Garland Series*.

Hurt, R. Douglas. *Agriculture and Slavery in Missouri's Little Dixie.* Columbia: University of Missouri Press, 1992.
A study of the seven-county region of central Missouri which contained almost one-fourth of the state's slave population. It is an attempt to discuss the relationship of slavery, economic development, rural white life, and agriculture. The discussion of slave management and control relates the brutality of the system and describes the racial attitudes of slavery's defenders. 334 pages with maps, a bibliography, and an index.

Johnston, James Hero. *Race Relations and Miscegenation in the South, 1776-1860.* Amherst: University of Massachusetts Press, 1970.
Originally written in 1937 as a doctoral dissertation at the University of Chicago, this work was not published until thirty-three years later. The author, an African American historian, details the relationships between white masters and their black mistresses and incorporates documentary evidence from his reading of petitions from emancipated slaves who wanted to remain in Virginia near their loved ones. A 1806 Virginia law, however, gave free blacks only one year to leave the state or face reenslavement and most petitioners were eventually expelled. Includes an interesting foreword by Winthrop Jordan and an index.

Jordan, Winthrop D., and Sheila Skemp, eds. *Race and Family in the Colonial South.* Jackson: University Press of Mississippi, 1987.
A collection of six essays plus an introduction by Jordan, this volume contains the papers presented at the Twelfth Annual Chancellor's Symposium in Southern History. The essays cover seventeenth and eighteenth century plantation life in Mississippi and French Louisiana. The essay by Patricia Galloway, "Talking with Indians: Interpreters and Diplomacy" (pages 109-130), is especially worth reading. 173 pages with notes and an index.

Joyner, Charles. *Down by the Riverside: A South Carolina Slave Community.* Urbana: University of Illinois Press, 1984.
A volume in the Blacks in the New World Series, edited by August Meier. Covering the period from 1830 to 1865, Joyner's study looks at All Saints Parish, a tiny South Carolina community, using evidence gathered from folklore, WPA interviews of the 1930's, wills, court

records, and songs. Joyner tries to discover the emotional texture of slave life by discussing dreams, hopes, and anxieties. 345 pages with a few pictures, many notes, and an index.

Killion, Ronald, and Charles Waller. *Slavery Time When I Was Chillun Down on Marster's Plantation: Interviews With Georgia Slaves.* Savannah, Ga.: Beehive Press, 1973.
Eighteen condensed narratives from the WPA collection with introductions by the authors. The many photographs makeup for the difficult reading based on verbatim transcriptions of interviews recorded by WPA staff members. The heavy southern dialect makes for difficult reading. 167 pages with dozens of well-reproduced photographs.

Kulikoff, Allan. *Tobacco and Slaves: The Development of Southern Cultures in the Chesapeake, 1680-1800.* Chapel Hill: University of North Carolina Press, 1986. Quantitative history presented in an extremely readable form. Describes the emergence of two societies: one free and racist, the other slave, but which also included a "free black" population that had no freedom. Free blacks sank to the bottom of society because of the racism of white society. The fear of social revolution pervaded white society and gave many slave owners uncomfortable and sleepless nights. 449 pages with maps, tables, and an index.

Lewis, Ronald L. *Coal, Iron, and Slaves: Industrial Slavery in Maryland and Virginia, 1715-1865.* Westport, Conn.: Greenwood Press, 1979.
A study of slavery in coal mines, the lumber industry, iron foundries, and fisheries. Examines the day-to-day patterns of human affairs in an urban, industrial environment. It made little difference in the lives of slaves. The owners were no more liberal or progressive in their treatment of slaves than were the most racist plantation owners. Both showed a fanatic devotion to white supremacy and the goodness of slavery. 283 pages with illustrations, seventeen tables, and an index.

Littlefield, Daniel. *Rice and Slaves: Ethnicity and the Slave Trade in Colonial South Carolina.* Urbana: University of Illinois Press, 1991.
Eighteenth century South Carolina slave owners had a more positive view of African culture and work habits than did their nineteenth century counterparts. They respected the intelligence and knowledge of their slaves and learned much from them about medicine and the growing of crops. Slaves were still property, of course, but they were not yet considered lazy, ignorant, and totally uncivilized. Unfortu-

nately, no explanation is provided for how the change of attitudes developed. 199 pages with a bibliography and an index.

McColley, Robert. *Slavery and Jeffersonian Virginia.* Urbana: University of Illinois Press, 1973.
Describes the influence of slavery on the life and thought of eighteenth century Virginia. Slavery was not declining during this period, as some historians had previously suggested, but was actually expanding. Many whites, including Thomas Jefferson, defended slavery on the basis of Africans' ignorance, their helplessness in face of the superiority of white culture, and their laziness (which seemed to be surmounted only when they were forced into the fields). Whites also defended slavery for economic reasons because they made huge profits from it. 227 pages with a bibliography and an index.

McGary, Howard, and Bill E. Lawson. *Between Slavery and Freedom: Philosophy and American Slavery.* Bloomington: Indiana University Press, 1992.
A brief collection of six essays by two philosophers commenting on their reading of slave narratives. They find that slavery was not pater-nalistic or humane and that Americans have failed to appreciate the terrible impact of slavery on its victims. Slaves who forgave their masters, the authors suggest, showed a lack of self-respect and honor. An unusual book because American philosophers have generally had little to say about history. 146 pages with notes, a short bibliography, and an index.

McLaurin, Melton A. *Celia: A Slave.* Athens: University of Georgia Press, 1991.
A short book that shows the true horrors of slave life. Celia, a slave in Callaway County, Missouri, was tried and hanged for murder of a white master who abused her. She was nineteen years old, the mother of two children, and may have been innocent. Documents Stanley Elkins' point that slaves were powerless to protect themselves from abuse and degradation. The psychic cost of such exploitation was incalculably damaging to African Americans. A book that can been read and used in high school and college classes. 148 pages with extensive notes, a bibliography, and an index.

MacLeod, Duncan J. *Slavery, Race, and the American Revolution.* Cambridge, England: Cambridge University Press, 1974.
MacLeod sees the American Revolution as a crucial event in the development of a consciously racist defense of slavery. If all men were

created equal, then slaves could not be men. Slavery was defended by pointing to the savagery, ignorance, and backwardness of the African character. Equality was justified only for civilized men. Equality and liberty could be denied to Africans because they had not reached the level of civilization required to benefit from those natural rights. 249 pages with a bibliography and an index.

Main, Gloria L. *Tobacco Colony: Life in Early Maryland, 1650-1720.* Princeton, N.J.: Princeton University Press, 1982.
Discusses the growth of slavery a relatively poor colony. The statistical analysis is well handled and easily understood. All whites supported the system and all would have owned slaves if they could have afforded them. Few whites showed any moral concerns over the institution and even though most free whites were little better off than slaves or the remaining indentured servants. This latter category of temporarily unfree whites disappeared as masters found that slaves were cheaper, reproduced themselves, and worked more steadily under constant fear of whipping. 326 pages with sixty-four tables, an extensive bibliography, and an index.

Malone, Ann Patton. *Sweet Chariot: Slave Family and Household Structure in Nineteenth Century Louisiana.* Chapel Hill: University of North Carolina Press, 1992.
Slave families were stable with many single-family households, usually headed by a female. Some statistics and rather confusing quantitative analysis. Families provided respite from long hours of labor and comfort and love when the pain of bondage grew too great. 369 pages with illustrations, two maps, thirty-five tables, extensive notes, a bibliography, and an index.

Miller, Randall M., ed. *"Dear Master": Letters of a Slave Family.* Ithaca, N.Y.: Cornell University Press, 1978.
A collection of letters from members of the Skipwith family of Virginia. Some had been freed in the 1820's and emigrated to Liberia while others had been sold to a new owner in Alabama. Describes conditions in all three places and provides an interesting contrast between slavery and freedom. From the largest collection of letters left by a slave family. Useful introductions provide an understanding of the different conditions and perspectives experienced by family members. 218 pages with illustrations, maps, and a bibliographical essay.

Mohr, Clarence L. *On the Threshold of Freedom: Masters and Slaves in Civil War Georgia.* Athens: University of Georgia Press, 1986.

Discusses the demise of slavery between 1859 and 1865. Embraces both black and white points of view. Whites trembled in fear at the thought of emancipation. Only in slavery could Africans be restrained from their savage, violent natures. An end to slavery meant an end to civilization. Saving it was worth a war. A well-written, informative survey. 397 pages with illustrations, maps, twenty-one tables, detailed notes, a bibliography, and an index.

Mooney, Chase C. *Slavery in Tennessee.* Westport, Conn.: Negro Universities Press, 1971.
An early state study originally published in 1957. Discusses the legal status of slaves, the antislavery movement in the state, the life of slaves, and the travails of fugitives. Uses census returns wisely and concludes that whites maintained slavery because they saw it as the only feasible solution to the race problem. Freedom would lead to race war. 250 pages with a statistical appendix and an index.

Nash, Gary B. *Race and Revolution.* Madison, Wisc.: Madison House, 1990.
Three essays on the origins of abolitionism in the pre-Revolutionary period, its failure resulting from lack of support for abolition after the war was concluded, and the effect of the American Revolution on the idea of equality. Originally delivered as the Merrill Jensen Lectures in Constitutional Studies, the text includes documents illustrating each essay. The documents consist of letters, speeches, editorial, contemporary abolitionist essays, and sample of pamphlet literature. 212 pages with notes, suggestions for further reading, and an index. Useful in advanced level courses.

Newton, James E., and Ronald L. Lewis, eds. *The Other Slaves: Mechanics, Artisans and Craftsmen.* Boston: G. K. Hall, 1978.
A collection of nineteen essays concerning the impact of industrialism upon skilled slaves. Robert Starobin, a Marxist scholar, contributed the very useful "Race Relations in Old South Industries" (pages 51-60). Masters in factories were just as hostile to blacks as were plantation owners. Also includes essays on labor in tobacco factories, the hemp industry, coal mining, and lumber mills. 245 pages.

Noël Hume, Ivor. *Martin's Hundred.* New York: Alfred A. Knopf, 1982.
Results of a five-year archeological study of a Virginia plantation in the Jamestown region based on excavations of bones and pottery. Contains more than one hundred illustrations, drawings, and photo-

graphs but only a very brief discussion of the lives of slaves. 343 pages with a bibliography.

Noonan, John T., Jr. *The Antelope: The Ordeal of the Recaptured Africans in the Administrations of James Monroe and John Quincy Adams.* Berkeley: University of California Press, 1977.
The ordeal of 280 slaves who mutinied on their way to Cuba, took over their ship, and tried to land in the United States. Presents a day-by-day account of their attempt to gain admission to the United States, which they were finally denied. 198 pages with notes and an index.

Osofsky, Gilbert, ed. *Puttin' on Ole Massa: The Slave Narratives of Henry Bibb, William Wells Brown, and Soloman Northrup.* New York: Harper & Row, 1969.
One of many collections of slave narratives. This one has a useful introduction on "The Significance of Slave Narratives," by the editor. Bibb and Brown were runaways who became leading figures in the abolitionist movement. Brown became a novelist, playwright, and lecturer, and Bibb edited "The Voice of the Fugitive" from Canada. 409 pages.

Otto, John S. *Cannon's Point Plantation, 1794-1860: Living Conditions and Status Patterns in the Old South.* Orlando, Fla.: Academic Press, 1984.
Part of the Studies in Historical Archaeology series, Otto's work includes brief essays on housing conditions, food, recreation, lifestyles, clothing, and tools used by slaves and their masters. The plantation was in the Sea Islands off the Georgia coast. 217 pages with a bibliography of archaeological sources, some statistics, drawings, and maps, with an index. As is true with most studies of material culture, this work is a bit dry and static.

Perdue, Charles L., Jr., Thomas E. Barden, and Robert K. Phillips, eds. *Weevils in the Wheat: Interviews With Virginia Ex-Slaves.* Charlottesville: University Press of Virginia, 1976.
Interviews with former slaves done by an all-black unit of the Virginia Writers' Project of the Works Progress Administration (WPA) between 1936 and 1938. More than three hundred elderly African Americans were questioned by interviewers, but more than half of the transcripts were later lost or destroyed. This book presents many of the surviving talks in their original dialect. Black interviewers probably received more accurate responses than did the whites sent out in other states. There are fewer expressions of love for "Old Master" here. The

photographs and the annotated bibliography of slave narratives make this volume quite useful. 405 pages with illustrations, notes, and an index.

Postell, William D. *The Health of Slaves on Southern Plantations.* Baton Rouge: Louisiana State University Press, 1951.
A book by a southern physician that finds the health of slaves comparable to the health of free people. Medical care on plantations was in accord with accepted practices. It was in the interest of owners to promote the health of slaves. For a contrasting view, see Todd L. Savitt's *Medicine and Slavery*, cited below. Includes an index, notes, and several illustrations and tables.

Quarles, Benjamin. *The Negro in the American Revolution.* Chapel Hill: University of North Carolina Press, 1961.
Quarles describes the role of African Americans who fought on the Patriot and the Loyalist sides, the aftermath of the war, and the war's effect on slavery in the North and the South. An interesting and extremely well-written study.

Raboteau, Albert J. *Slave Religion: The "Invisible Institution" in the Antebellum South.* New York: Oxford University Press, 1979.
The best survey of African and Christian religion in the African American slave community. This well-written study presents an excellent analysis of the interweaving of ideas that led to the eventual emergence of an African American religion.

Ransom, Roger L. *Conflict and Compromise: The Political Economy of Slavery, Emancipation, and the American Civil War.* Cambridge, England: Cambridge University Press, 1989.
An economic history beginning with the Missouri Compromise of 1820 and concluding with the ending of Reconstruction. Ransom's work includes a brief discussion of racism. Unfortunately, his work provides somewhat less than compelling reading, although the statistical information contained in its numerous tables, charts, and graphs is easily absorbed. 317 pages with a bibliography and an index.

Reidy, Joseph P. *From Slavery to Agrarian Capitalism in the Cotton Plantation South: Central Georgia, 1800-1880.* Chapel Hill: University of North Carolina Press, 1992.
One of the few books to bridge the pre- and post-Civil War eras. Examines a typical cotton region over several generations concentrating on economics. Profound changes took place after the war because

of the expanding world market for cotton, but racism kept blacks from gaining too much from these changes. 360 pages with three maps, a bibliography, notes, and an index.

Ripley, C. Peter. *Slaves and Freedmen in Civil War Louisiana.* Baton Rouge: Louisiana State University Press, 1976.
The early reconquest of Louisiana by Union forces made the programs and agencies created in the state models for postwar attempts to deal with freedmen. The Bureau of Negro Labor and Education set up in the state presaged the Freedmen's Bureau. The Army, from 1862 to 1865, placed severe restrictions on black advancements and liberties during the war and demonstrated the extremely conservative racial attitudes of northerners. 237 pages with six table, an essay on sources, and an index.

Robinson, Donald L. *Slavery in the Structure of American Politics, 1765-1820.* New York: Harcourt Brace Jovanovich, 1971.
Slavery could not have been eliminated from American society except by war. It could not have been prevented by different decisions by the Framers of the Constitution or any other political leaders because without slavery the South would have walked out of the Constitutional Convention and there would have been no union at all. 564 pages with four tables, notes, and an index.

Rutman, Darrett B., and Anita H. Rutman. *A Place in Time: Middlesex County, Virginia, 1650-1750.* New York: W. W. Norton, 1984.
Based on more than twelve thousand biographies of Middlesex County residents, free and slave, created from a statistical analysis of census and court records. At the root of the great violence against blacks was a history of suspicion, distrust, and fear. The larger the number of Africans grew, "this strange and alien race," according to one slave owner, the greater the fear and the more repressive slavery became. 287 pages with illustrations, maps, and extensive notes. A companion volume, *A Place in Time: Explications*, contains the underlying statistical evidence upon which the first volume depends.

Savitt, Todd L. *Medicine and Slavery: The Diseases and Health Care of Blacks in Antebellum Virginia.* Urbana: University of Illinois Press, 1978.
Savitt discusses the health and working conditions of slaves and provides an interesting history of the relationship between black health and white society from 1775 to 1861. Considers the effects of malaria, worms, yellow fever, dysentery, and other killer diseases on those seen

as the lowest members of society. Treatment by white doctors was based on the need to keep machines—in this case, slaves—in good working order. The author is a physician and a historian. 332 pages with nine illustrations, twenty-seven tables and figures, a note on sources, and index.

Schwarz, Philip J. *Twice Condemned: Slaves and the Criminal Laws of Virginia, 1705-1865.* Baton Rouge: Louisiana State University Press, 1988.
A study of the brutality of slavery and the even greater brutality of the criminal laws written to deal with free blacks and slaves who violated standards of justice.

Sellers, James B. *Slavery in Alabama.* University: University of Alabama Press, 1950.
A early study of the institution covering ground from French territorial times to the end of the Civil War. Sellers sees slaves as responding to masters with a childlike trust, a typical view among historians when this book was written. Chapters of runaways, free blacks, crimes, work habits, and the lifestyle of the planter class. Has been superceded by subsequent studies. 426 pages with five illustrations and an index.

Smith, Julia Floyd. *Slavery and Plantation Growth in Antebellum Florida, 1821-1860.* Gainesville: University of Florida Press, 1973.
According to Smith, slavery in Florida was quite benign, and slaves and masters got along well, with the owners making a huge amount of money every year. Discusses slave-trading, labor of field hands, slaves and the law, and the economics of the plantation system. 249 pages with a few illustrations, a bibliography, and an index.

_____. *Slavery and Rice Culture in Low Country Georgia, 1750-1860.* Knoxville: University of Tennessee Press, 1985.
Explores the culture of white rice growers and their attitudes toward African slaves. The author believes that owners cared for and showed concern for their slaves and that house servants generally were treated humanely. The mulatto offspring of slave-master relationships also received humane treatment. Smith's relatively benign view of the system has been contradicted by many other studies. 266 pages with thirty-six illustrations, eight tables, a bibliography and an index.

Sobel, Mechal. *The World They Made Together: Black and White Values in Eighteenth Century Virginia.* Princeton, N.J.: Princeton University Press, 1987.

A study of attitudes toward work, time, and the world of nature. Blacks and whites lived together in great intimacy in the 1700's and deeply influenced one another's view of reality. Although they differed greatly, African values concerning family, work, and religion influenced the development of white attitudes and values. 364 pages with forty-four pictures, a bibliography, extensive notes, and an index. Written by a historian, this work is an interesting, perceptive study that is occasionally marred by its reliance on sociological jargon.

Southern, Eileen. *The Music of Black Americans: A History.* 2d ed. New York: W. W. Norton, 1983.
A massive textbook covering all aspects of black music from its African origins to popular music of the 1980's. Good chapters on music of slaves, songs of the Underground Railroad, plantation work songs, spirituals, hymns, and other religious music. Southern demonstrates a perceptive concern for the social, political, and economic forces that helped shape the music. 602 pages with illustrations, a bibliography, a discography, and an index.

Starobin, Robert S. *Industrial Slavery in the Old South.* New York: Oxford University Press, 1970.
A study of slave labor in southern industries from 1790 to 1861. Particular interest is paid to conditions in mining, lumbering, construction, and transportation. Slavery made businesses more profitable than free labor since it cost much less. Conditions of slaves in cities and industrial surroundings were harsh and grim. Resistance was difficult and most slaves sought to accommodate themselves to the difficulties of their condition. 320 pages with four tables, notes, and an index.

Stuckey, Sterling. *Slave Culture: Nationalist Theory and the Foundations of Black America.* New York: Oxford University Press, 1987.
Stuckey finds that even after the slave experience most blacks remained decidedly African in their culture. Based on a study of folklore, his work seeks to discover how a unified African American culture was formed out of the many peoples of Africa brought over as slaves. Includes descriptions of slave rituals and how they bound Africans together against a common foe, the white man. Stuckey sees slavery as a force for detribalization in America and a creator of unity. There is a final chapter on the music of singer Paul Robeson and a lengthy discussion of W. E. B. Du Bois. As with most folklorists, Stuckey assumes that the stories were as important as the real events. 425 pages with thirty tables and charts, extensive notes and an index.

Tate, Thad W. *The Negro in Eighteenth Century Williamsburg.* Charlottesville: University Press of Virginia, 1980.
A brief description of the lives of slaves and servants in Virginia from
the introduction of African Americans to the aftermath of Bacon's
Rebellion. Considers religion and culture in slave life.

_____, ed. *Race and Family in the Colonial South: Essays.* Jackson:
University Press of Mississippi, 1987.
A brief collection of essays by historians presented at a conference on
the topic of race and family. The essays consider the usual themes of
struggle, survival, and change.

Taylor, Orville W. *Negro Slavery in Arkansas.* Durham, N.C.: Duke
University Press, 1958.
An interesting survey of slavery from the 1720's to 1863 by a black
historian. The existence of slavery depended on force and fear. Interesting discussions of crime and punishment, health care, slave religion,
and the role of overseers in keeping slaves passive. 282 pages with five
illustrations and an index. The only history of slavery in this state.

Van DeBurg, William L. *The Slave Drivers: Black Agricultural Labor in
the Antebellum South.* Westport, Conn.: Greenwood Press, 1979.
Black slave drivers had to decide whether to follow the will of their
owners or side with their fellow Africans. The drivers most often chose
to follow their fellows rather than their masters. Black slave drivers
experienced the same deprivations and felt the same hostility toward
their masters as black field hands did. They were sold, whipped, or
demoted according to the whim of their masters. Nevertheless, they
refused to be crushed by their burdens and maintained a sense of
dignity and humanity. 202 pages with a brief bibliography and extensive notes.

Vernon, Amelia Wallace. *African Americans at Mars Bluff, South Carolina.* Baton Rouge: Louisiana State University Press, 1993.
A clearly written study of a farming community in the South Carolina
pine belt. Based on taped interviews and oral history but includes much
information on rice cultivation, slave religions, slave language, and
memories of slavery. 309 pages with fifty-two drawings and figures,
nine maps, an extensive bibliography, notes, and an index.

Wade, Richard C. *Slavery in the Cities: The South, 1820-1860.* New York:
Oxford University Press, 1964.

A classic study of slave life in urban environments that now appears dated when compared to the work by Dale Goldin cited above. According to Wade, the freedom of the city helped erode slavery as contact with free people generated a rebellious spirit among urban slaves. Masters found it quite difficult to establish their control. In the country, the physical isolation of slaves kept blacks apart and prevented conspiracies and rebellion. Such was not the case in southern cities. 340 pages with extensive notes, a bibliographical essay, and an index.

Webber, Thomas L. *Deep Like Rivers: Education in the Slave Quarter Community, 1831-1865.* New York: W. W. Norton, 1978.
What did whites want slaves to learn? What did slaves learn? From whom did slaves learn what they learned? A study of secular and religious training for slaves. Includes an interesting comparison of slave education and schooling for American Indians. Try as they might, whites could not get control of black or Native American minds. Slaves created a new and separate culture combining their African past with southern slave experience. A study based on folklore and narratives. 339 pages with extensive notes and an index.

Wiethoff, William E. *A Peculiar Humanism: The Judicial Advocacy of Slavery in High Courts of the Old South, 1820-1850.* Athens: University of Georgia Press, 1996.
Presents an assessment of southern state judges and their defense of slavery and the mistreatment of slaves. Many judges went out of their way to defend the slave system and proclaim its civilizing and humanizing power. 247 pages with notes and an index.

Wood, Betty. *Slavery in Georgia, 1730-1775.* Athens: University of Georgia Press, 1984.
Georgia originally tried to ban slavery when it became a colony in 1732. By the 1760's, however, a slave system flourished and free labor was largely abandoned. Proslavery advocates stressed the economic advantages of slavery in comparison with free labor and that argument won. 254 pages with notes and an index.

Wood, Peter. *Black Majority: Negroes in Colonial South Carolina from 1670 Through the Stono Rebellion.* New York: Alfred A. Knopf, 1974.
Wood stresses African contributions to science, medicine, and culture in the only colony with a black majority. His popularly written account provides a detailed discussion of the origins of a slave revolt in 1739. 346 pages with tables, charts, extensive notes, and a bibliographical note.

Wright, Donald R. *African Americans in the Colonial Era from African Origins Through the American Revolution.* Arlington Heights, Ill.: Harlan Davidson, 1990.

A brief survey of the subject that describes the differing views of slavery from its New World origins through the 1780's.

Chapter 4

FREE BLACKS AND SLAVE REVOLTS

FREE BLACKS

Alexander, Adele Logan. *Ambiguous Lives: Free Women of Color in Rural Georgia, 1789-1879.* Fayetteville: University of Arkansas Press, 1991. The story of the Hunt family of Hancock County, Georgia, members of "the privileged class" of free blacks. The Hunts had been free since 1789, acquired property, attended college, and lived in a racist society that subjected family members to discrimination, hostility, and great fear. Whatever they did, they were still seen as members of an inferior race and relegated to second-class status. 268 pages charts, maps, photographs, notes, a bibliography, and an index.

Banner, Melvin E. *The Black Pioneer in Michigan. Volume 1: Flint and Genesee County.* Midland, Mich.: Pendell, 1973. A brief collection from a series of newspaper articles tracing the early history of black families and churches in central Michigan. The series originally appeared in 1964 in the *Bronze Reporter*, a newspaper published in Flint, Michigan. 89 pages with photographs.

Berlin, Ira. *Slaves Without Masters: The Free Negro in the Antebellum South.* New York: Pantheon Books, 1974. The first general survey of free blacks to appear, this work tells the story of discrimination and prejudice as free blacks remained at the bottom of the social order. They were despised by whites, more so than slaves, because slaves were at least in their proper place. Free blacks violated white conceptions of the social order; if they succeeded, it would mean blacks were equal to whites, and that was impossible. Berlin shows how they lived, worked, and educated themselves while suffering verbal and physical abuse. 423 pages with a list of manuscript sources, notes, tables, and an index.

Brasseaux, Carl A., Keith Fontenot, and Claude F. Oubre. *Creoles of Color in the Bayou Country.* Jackson: University Press of Mississippi, 1994. A history of Creole society from its eighteenth century origins to modern times. Creoles were free people of color resulting from mixed marriages when Louisiana was still Spanish and later French. During this time, a three-tiered society emerged: white, free colored, and slave. Creoles did not want to be seen as black, because free Africans had been segregated by law since 1724. Creoles imitated white society by becoming Catholic, speaking French, and owning slaves. When Louisiana became part of the United States shortly after the conclusion of the American Revolution, the three tiers disappeared because white America saw only two colors—black and white. All "inferior" blacks were subjected to segregation. 174 pages with illustrations and an index.

Brown, Letitia Woods. *Free Negroes in the District of Columbia, 1790-1846.* New York: Oxford University Press, 1972.
Part of Oxford's Urban Life in America series, Brown's study takes a brief look at the treatment of free people of color in the nation's capital. Despite severe discrimination and racial barriers, they managed to create a diverse and stable, though economically depressed, community. The only jobs available were in manual labor and domestic service. Segregation was extreme. The separate black community did produce its own doctors, teachers, and ministers, primarily because no one else would serve in these capacities. A middle class of professionals did develop despite discrimination. 226 pages with notes and an index.

Campbell, Penelope. *Maryland in Africa: The Maryland State Colonization Society, 1831-1857.* Urbana: University of Illinois Press, 1991.
Not all free blacks stayed in the United States. The American Colonization Society, founded in 1817 by whites, believed that the best solution to the race problem in the United States was repatriation of slaves to their African homeland. Thus, they bought land in West Africa (modern Liberia) from an African emperor and began buying slave contracts. The story of the problems faced by colonizationists is related in this book. 264 pages with a bibliography and an index.

Cohen, David W., and Jack P. Greene. *Neither Slave nor Free: The Freedmen of African Descent in the Slave Societies of the New World.* Baltimore: The Johns Hopkins University Press, 1972.
Ten essays from a symposium on "The Role of the Free Black and Free Mulatto in Slave Societies of the New World." Covers treatment in South, Central, and North America. H. Hoetink contributes a comparative essay (pages 59-84) on experiences in Surinam, Cuba, and Brazil,

and Eugene Genovese writes on the experience of free blacks in slave states (pages 258-77). 344 pages with tables and an index.

Curry, Leonard P. *The Free Black in Urban America, 1800-1850: The Shadow of a Dream.* Chicago: University of Chicago Press, 1981.
White Americans did not allow free blacks to share fully in the dream of prosperity and justice for all. They limited access to education, closed many occupations to freed slaves, and denied them adequate housing. *De facto* segregation, resulting from attitudes and behavior, long predated *de jure*, segregation by law. Despite the dehumanizing treatment, free blacks held on to a shadow of the dream of freedom and lived lives of dignity and bravery. 346 pages with thirty-five charts, seventeen figures giving population distributions in major cities, notes, and an index.

Dykstra, Robert R. *Bright Radical Star: Black Freedom and White Supremacy on the Hawkeye Frontier.* Cambridge, Mass.: Harvard University Press, 1993.
White racism existed in a state with a black population of less than 1 percent in the 1880 census. Whites simply did not want blacks around, whether they were slave or free. Iowa whites from 1833 to 1880 reacted not to the fact of a black presence but to the prospect of it. Dykstra provides an analysis of elections in which Iowans denied free blacks the right to vote and supported legislation designed to keep African Americans from settling in the state. 348 pages with nine maps, a statistical appendix, notes, and an index.

Egerton, Douglas R. *Gabriel's Rebellion: The Virginia Slave Conspiracies of 1800 and 1802.* Chapel Hill: University of North Carolina Press, 1993.
Gabriel, a highly skilled blacksmith and a literate free black, organized a revolt that sought to destroy the economic power of the white planter elite. He hoped that poor whites would join his revolt, but underestimated the power of racial loyalty in white society. Had his revolt succeeded instead of being betrayed by informants, slavery might have been brought to an early end and the course of American history would have been radically changed. 262 pages with notes and an index.

Franklin, John Hope. *The Free Negro in North Carolina, 1790-1860.* New York: Russell & Russell, 1969.
Originally published in 1943, this first work by the eminent historian traces the development of segregation before the Civil War. Whites showed little humanity or wisdom in their legal and social relationships

with free blacks. The free population lived on the margins of society, an unwanted people who became increasingly frustrated and restless. 271 pages with an index.

Hirsch, Arnold R., and Joseph Logsdon, eds. *Creole New Orleans: Race and Americanization.* Baton Rouge: Louisiana University Press, 1992. Six essays on Afro-Creole culture covering the period from colonization to the 1980's. Creoles, who were people of mixed race, rejected identification with the city's black community, free and slave. The coming of segregation for all people of color relegated Creoles to lives of segregation and second-class citizenship. The racial divide continued during the 1980's, even after the election of a Creole mayor. The defeat of legal segregation did not unify New Orlean's colored community. 334 pages with an index.

Horton, James Oliver. *Free People of Color: Inside the African American Community.* Washington, D.C.: Smithsonian Institution Press, 1993. Chapters on life in the nineteenth century North and South. In "Race and Ethnicity in Mid-Nineteenth Century Buffalo" (pages 170-183), authors James Horton and Hartmut Keil compare the relations between Germans, Irish, and African Americans. They find German-black relations more harmonious that Irish-black relations because the latter groups competed more for lower level jobs. The Irish saw themselves as "victims" of prejudice who had to protect what they had, usually unskilled jobs, while Germans, being higher on the economic scale, felt less threatened by African Americans. Germans hardly believed in equality, they just had less contact with blacks because they knew they could not compete for the jobs held by skilled German laborers. 238 pages with notes and an index.

Jackson, Luther Porter. *Free Negro Labor and Property Holding in Virginia, 1830-1860.* Reprint. New York: Russell & Russell, 1971. Originally published in 1942, Jackson's work contains a discussion of prevailing attitudes and lifestyles. Whites wanted to keep the number of free blacks as small as possible. An 1806 law allowed reenslavement of any African American who remained in the state for more than a year. Fear and hatred grew rapidly in the aftermath of slaves rebellions. In 1831, after Nat Turner's bloody uprising, whites flooded the legislature with petitions asking for the removal of all free "Negroes." In 1838, the Virginia legislature banned public education for free blacks. As a group, free blacks had no place in a society wedded to racial supremacy and slavery. 270 pages with and index.

Johnson, Michael P., and James L. Roark. *Black Masters: A Free Family of Color in the Old South.* New York: W. W. Norton, 1984.
The story of William Ellison, one of five hundred thousand free blacks in the South. Born a slave of mixed race in 1790, he eventually bought his freedom in 1816 and became one of the wealthiest persons of color in the United States. Ellison owned a large cotton plantation in South Carolina and owned many slaves. 422 pages with maps, illustrations, and an index.

_____, eds. *No Chariot Let Down: Charleston's Free People of Color on the Eve of the Civil War.* Chapel Hill: University of North Carolina Press, 1984.
Covering the period from 1849 to 1864, this work contains the correspondence of the Ellisons, a family of free blacks living in South Carolina. Includes a discussion of the 1859 Charleston enslavement crisis, when authorities attempted to enslave all free blacks who could not prove their freedom. Despite its wealth and success, the Ellison family met with great prejudice and hostility. 174 pages with illustrations and an index.

Koger, Larry. *Black Slaveowners: Free Black Slave Masters in South Carolina, 1790-1860.* Jefferson, N.C.: McFarland, 1985.
An African American historian finds that free black masters owned slaves for the same reasons as whites, to make money. More than 83 percent of black slaveholders were mulattoes, while 90 percent of slaves were African. Black owners were darker copies of their white counterparts, but they still suffered discrimination because of their race. 286 pages with ten tables, notes, and an index.

Lapp, Rudolph M. *Blacks in Gold Rush California.* New Haven, Conn.: Yale University Press, 1977.
In 1849, hundreds of free blacks joined thousands of other gold seekers in northern California. Some white southerners brought their slaves with them to help dig for gold in the mines. By 1850, blacks formed about 1 percent of California's population. Despite their small numbers, blacks were subjected to violence and discrimination and were a despised and oppressed minority. After California achieved statehood, blacks were denied the right to vote. 321 pages with illustrations, notes, a bibliography, and an index.

Litwack, Leon F. *North of Slavery: The Negro in the Free States, 1790-1860.* Chicago: University of Chicago Press, 1961.

A masterful survey of the important distinctions between freedom and slavery. In the North, blacks were free and were not subject to the whims of a white master. Although victimized by racial prejudice and discrimination, free blacks could still advance their political and economic position. Whites subjected blacks in the North to anger, hatred, bitterness, and charges of inequality but freedom still offered more than slavery. 318 pages with an index.

Miller, Floyd J. *The Search for a Black Nationality: Black Emigration and Colonization, 1787-1863.* Urbana: University of Illinois Press, 1975.
Many blacks living in the North in the 1780's believed they could never achieve freedom and equality in the United States. Only emigration to Africa appeared to offer them the opportunity to gain dignity and respect. There, they could bring with them the fruits of Western learning and religion and help "civilize" the "backward" peoples of their ancient homeland. The idea of emigration never lost its appeal to those slaves and former slaves who were totally alienated from their oppressors. Martin A. Delany, a black preacher and abolitionist, proposed the creation of a black nation in either Haiti or West Africa. This nation was to be made up of black people from throughout the world—a dream never achieved but one that still brought hope to many of the oppressed. 295 pages with an essay on sources and an index.

Mills, Gary B. *The Forgotten People: Cane River's Creoles of Color.* Baton Rouge: Louisiana State University Press, 1977.
Another study of a group, neither black nor white, that struggled against prejudice in a small area of Louisiana. The Creoles on the Cane River were of a mixed African, French, and Spanish heritage. Called mulattoes, a French and Spanish word derived from "mule," the Creoles considered themselves superior to blacks, but were considered black by whites and suffered from discrimination. To the colored population on the Cane River, the notion that there was a bond of color tying people together seemed preposterous. 277 pages with maps, photographs, genealogical charts, a bibliography, and an index.

Nash, Gary B. *Forging Freedom: The Formation of Philadelphia's Black Community, 1720-1840.* Cambridge, Mass.: Harvard University Press, 1988.
An account of how a spirit of racial harmony in the 1790's, resulting from the continuing appeal of revolutionary ideals of liberty, was transformed into open hatred of African Americans just a generation later. Competition for jobs created some of the hatred as did the

growing influence of doctrines of white supremacy. 354 pages with illustrations, notes, and an index.

Nash, Gary B., and Jean R. Soderlund. *Freedom by Degrees: Emancipation in Pennsylvania and Its Aftermath.* New York: Oxford University Press, 1991.
Many colonists who talked of freedom and justice refused to condemn slavery. Benjamin Franklin, for example, owned slaves and did not free them until his death. He did find slavery objectionable, but on economic rather than moral grounds. Free laborers worked harder and produced more because their own self-interest was involved. Since slaves worked only for their masters, business suffered because slaves had little incentive to produce more. The antislavery movement in Pennsylvania began with the Society of Friends (Quakers) in the 1750's. During the American Revolution, Pennsylvania became the first state to ban slavery. Nevertheless, free blacks continued to suffer economic hardship because of white prejudice. 249 pages with notes and an index.

Nichols, Charles, ed. *Black Men in Chains: Narratives by Escaped Slaves.* New York: Lawrence Hill, 1972.
Sixteen narratives excerpted from autobiographies and diaries introduced by the editor. Covers the period from 1745, when Gustavas Vassa escaped from the South, to the 1850's, including the recollections of William Parker, a runaway who eventually fled to Canada. Nat Turner's "Confession" and parts of Frederick Douglass' *Autobiography* are also included. 315 pages.

Piersen, William D. *Black Yankees: The Development of an Afro-American Subculture in Eighteenth-Century New England.* Amherst: University of Massachusetts Press, 1988.
Describes the process of cultural change involved in the creation of an African American community in the free and slave North before the American Revolution. Written from the view of African Americans, the book describes how African values were maintained through folklore and folk wisdom. 237 pages with a statistical appendix and an index.

Porter, Kenneth Wiggins. *The Negro on the Frontier.* New York: Arno Press, 1971.
A collection of essays by an African American historian covering the period from 1529 to 1909. Topics include relations between blacks and Native Americans, blacks as cowboys, and black soldiers in Texas and

Indian territory. Essays originally appeared in the *Journal of Negro History*. 530 pages.

Schweninger, Loren. *Black Property Owners in the South, 1790-1915.* Urbana: University of Illinois Press, 1990.
Tens of thousands of free blacks, out of a total of five hundred thousand, made impressive gains in acquisition of property and land. Focuses on the values, attitudes, and ideals of this elite. Successful free blacks showed a growing disgust with white society and one wrote that even free Africans had nothing to look forward to in the South except "death, hell, and the grave." No matter how prosperous they became, blacks would remain less than a man in the eyes of even the most ignorant whites. The achievements of free blacks, on the other hand, made a mockery of racial inferiority. 425 pages with thirty-nine tables, six figures, a select bibliography, and an index.

_____, ed. *From Tennessee Slave to St. Louis Entrepreneur: The Auto-biography of James Thomas.* Columbia: University of Missouri Press, 1984.
The story of a slave barber who saved enough money to buy his own freedom in 1841. Comments on the cruelty of white society and the shared pain of slaves and free blacks. Despite Thomas' success in real estate, banking, and other business affairs, whites still saw him as a member of an inferior race. Contains a foreword by John Hope Franklin. 225 pages with a index.

Smith, Billy G., and Richard Wojtowicz, eds. *Blacks Who Stole Them-selves: Advertisements for Runaways in "The Pennsylvania Gazette," 1728-1790.* Philadelphia: University of Pennsylvania Press, 1989.
Three hundred advertisements and drawings of 364 runaways repro-duced exactly as they appeared in Pennsylvania's leading newspaper. An introduction written by the editors provides background informa-tion and a quantitative analysis of the characteristics of fugitives. Most were young, male, and had some skills. 222 pages with a glossary, notes, and an index.

Staudenraus, P. J. *The African Colonization Movement, 1816-1865.* New York: Columbia University Press, 1961.
Staudenraus provides a history of the American Colonization Society (ACS) founded in 1817. Members fought the "social evil," not of slavery but of the presence of a socially inferior and repressed "race" of savages in North America. Slavery was a sin against God, so it had to be ended. Africans, however, could not remain in the states because

they threatened the peace and stability of society. Removal to Africa, after the purchase of their freedom by the ACS, would restore freedmen to their homeland and save America from a race war. 323 pages with notes and an index.

Sterkx, Herbert E. *The Free Negro in Antebellum Louisiana.* Rutherford, N.J.: Farleigh Dickinson University Press, 1972.
Covers the experience of free people of color in rural communities and New Orleans. Sterkx's study finds prejudice, discrimination, and fear everywhere. His findings repeat the message of all studies of free blacks: They were hated, despised, and relegated to the bottom of society. White supremacists could not accept even the idea of black equality.

Van Sertima, Ivan, ed. *African Presence in Early America.* New Brunswick, N.J.: Transaction Publishers, 1992.
Twelve essays originally published in the December, 1986, issue of *Journal of African Civilizations* on "Egypto-Nubian Presences in Ancient Mexico." Finds evidence of African influences in facial sculptures found in pre-Columbian America. Also includes Leo Wiener's "Africa and the Discovery of America," originally published in *The Journal of Negro History* in 1920. Wiener speculates on the outcome of trading voyages made by the Mandingo-Songhay empires into the Atlantic and the possibility that some ships from Africa landed in Brazil long before Europeans set foot in the New World. Includes Van Sertima's address to the Smithsonian Institution in 1991, in which the archaeologist suggests an African presence as long ago as the Bronze Age, 900 B.C. 318 pages with photographs, maps, and an index.

_____. *They Came Before Columbus.* New York: Random House, 1977.
According to Van Sertima, black people from Africa had reached Mexico more than two thousand years before Columbus. They left behind sculptures, mainly great stone heads, that could only have come from Africa, according to the author's interpretation of the archaeological evidence.

Voegeli, V. Jacque. *Free But Not Equal: The Midwest and the Negro During the Civil War.* Chicago: University of Chicago Press, 1967.
Midwestern whites shared the view of other white Americans that Africans were innately inferior. States from Ohio to Michigan and Illinois were determined to maintain white supremacy. Slavery had to be ended, of course, since it was a sin, but freedmen had to be kept in the South. 215 pages with notes and an index.

Walker, James W. St. G. *The Black Loyalists: The Search for a Promised Land in Nova Scotia and Sierra Leone, 1783-1870.* New York: Dalhousie University Press, 1976.
Blacks who fought with the British during the American Revolution were guaranteed freedom. After an failed attempt to set up a community in Nova Scotia, many of the eight thousand freedmen resettled in Sierra Leone on the West Coast of Africa where they helped established that British colony in its earliest and most dangerous years. 438 pages with a bibliography and an index.

Warner, Lee H. *Free Men in an Age of Servitude: Three Generations of a Black Family.* Lexington: University Press of Kentucky, 1992.
The story of the Proctor family: Antonio, an illiterate former slave who became a military hero; his son George, who went to California with the Forty-Niners and acquired some wealth; and his son John, who became a leader of the Republican Party in Florida and a state legislator. Despite these accomplishments, society denied the Proctors the prosperity and happiness they deserved. Racist attitudes among whites prevented them from achieving even greater heights. A painstakingly put together book based on deed books, court records, and government documents. 168 pages with notes, a bibliography, and an index.

White, Shane. *Somewhat More Independent: The End of Slavery in New York City, 1770-1810.* Athens: University of Georgia Press, 1991.
What did it mean to be black and living in New York City at the end of the 1700's and how was emancipation brought about? White also describes what freedom meant for African Americans. Generally, as was true in the South free blacks lived at the edge of society and worked in the lowest paying jobs. Discrimination was constant. 278 pages with notes, tables, maps, figures, and an index.

Wikramanayake, Marina. *A World in Shadow: The Free Black in Antebellum South Carolina.* Columbia: University of South Carolina Press, 1973.
A description of life at the edge, on the bottom of society, because of racism, discrimination and the constant fear among whites that freedom for African Americans would generally lead to race war.

Wilson, Carol. *Freedom at Risk: The Kidnapping of Free Blacks in America, 1780-1865.* Lexington: University Press of Kentucky, 1994.
Kidnapping was an all-too-common practice and a constant threat to free blacks, even those livi g in the North. Kidnappers physically abused and terrorized their captives and forced them to return to the

South. Whites accepted kidnapping as a way of enslaving free blacks without admitting responsibility. It served as a reminder to free blacks that they were not slaves, but they certainly were black and could be made a slave in a instant. It is impossible to estimate the numbers of kidnapped free blacks, but it was easily in the thousands. 177 pages with a bibliography, notes, and an index.

Windley, Lathan A. *Runaway Slave Advertisements: A Documentary History from the 1730's to 1790.* 4 vols. Westport, Conn.: Greenwood Press, 1983.
A documentary collection of several thousand runaway slave advertisements from weekly newspapers in Virginia, North Carolina, Maryland, South Carolina, and Georgia. These advertisements present a portrait of runaways in the eighteenth century and contain a wealth of information on sex, age, height, size, occupation, speech patterns, and physical defects. There is no interpretation, merely raw data. Includes a general index.

Zilversmit, Arthur. *The First Emancipation: The Abolition of Slavery in the North.* Chicago: University of Chicago Press, 1967.
A state-by-state survey of emancipation starting in 1715 and ending in 1804. Non-slaveholders opposed slavery in the North because slaves were supposedly not as productive as free laborers. Northern masters who found slavery very profitable vigorously opposed abolition, but they lost out to the idea of free labor and moral opposition by some churches to holding other people in bondage. 262 pages with a statistical appendix and an index.

SLAVE REVOLTS

Aptheker, Herbert. *American Negro Slave Revolts.* New York: Columbia University Press, 1943.
America's leading Marxist historian looks for slave revolts and finds many. Later historians believe he exaggerated the extent and number of rebellions. Revolts were just too dangerous and without weapons almost impossible. Still, this is a useful survey and interesting view of slave society and history. 416 pages with an index.

Davis, Thomas J. *A Rumor of Revolt: The "Great Negro Plot" in Colonial New York.* New York: Free Press, 1985.

In 1741, a white mob in New York City burned thirteen black men to death at the stake, and hanged twenty-one others, including two white men and two white women. The whites were charged with organizing a plot to overthrow the government, and influencing the African Americans to set fires and rob stores. Blacks made up about 20 percent of the city's population of eleven thousand and most were slaves. This study is based on court records that demonstrated that the slaves had talked about destroying white society. 320 pages with notes and an index.

Gara, Larry. *The Liberty Line: The Legend of the Underground Railroad.* Lexington: University Press of Kentucky, 1961.
A general history of the railroad—how it operated, who was involved, and what the results were. Well written and interesting.

Lofton, John. *Denmark Vesey's Revolt: The Slave Plot That Lit a Fuse to Fort Sumter.* Kent, Ohio: Kent State University Press, 1983.

_____. *Insurrection in South Carolina: The Turbulent World of Denmark Vesey.* Yellow Springs, Ohio: Antioch Press, 1964.
Two studies of a failed revolt, the reasons for it, and the consequences for American history.

Mullin, Gerald W. *Flight and Rebellion: Slave Resistance in Eighteenth Century Virginia.* New York: Oxford University Press, 1972.
The story of Gabriel's Rebellion in 1800 is included. The evolution of a slave society and methods of resistance. Discusses free blacks and fugitives and how Africans were made into slaves. Based on a reading of newspapers and runaway slave advertisements, this study describes the psychological differences between runaways and those who stayed. Many runaways stuttered, an indication of severe abuse of the slave population. 219 pages with maps, a bibliography, extensive notes, and an index.

Mullin, Michael. *Africa in America: Slave Acculturation and Resistance in the American South and the British Caribbean, 1736-1831.* Urbana: University of Illinois Press, 1992.
A comparison of rebellions in the United States, including Nat Turner's in 1831, and the largest rebellion in the New World, that in Jamaica that same year. The Jamaican uprising led to more than five hundred deaths, more than ten times the number of people killed in Turner's Rebellion. Why did most slaves never rebel? Who did rebel? What were the values and ideas expressed by the rebels? Most slaves were so

terribly dehumanized by their experience they did not have the resilience needed to rebel. Those who did rebel, mostly Creoles or mulattoes, had some hope for a better future. 412 pages with twelve illustrations, fourteen maps, notes, a bibliography, and an index.

Oates, Stephen B. *The Fires of Jubilee: Nat Turner's Fierce Rebellion.* New York: Harper & Row, 1975.
A popular, well-written history of the largest slave revolt in American history.

Tragle, Henry Irving. *The Southhampton Slave Revolt of 1831: A Compilation of Source Material.* Amherst: University of Massachusetts Press, 1971.
A useful collection of original documents, including court records, newspaper accounts, and eyewitness reports.

Chapter 5

RACE AND THE WHITE MIND BEFORE
THE CIVIL WAR

Abbott, Richard H. *Cotton and Capital: Boston Businessmen and Anti-slavery Reform, 1854-1868.* Amherst: University of Massachusetts Press, 1991.
Ending slavery would bestow significant benefits upon white Americans because free labor was superior to slave. A free-labor economy, one in which all men could advance by their own efforts, produced more than a slave system because slaves did not work to increase there own wealth. Blacks, of course, were not yet ready for total freedom but they would be better off free and working for themselves than for a master. Racists could support antislavery efforts. Freedom would create opportunities for economic equality. Social and political equality would wait for a later day, if ever. 294 pages with a bibliography, notes, and an index.

Allmendinger, David F., Jr. *Ruffin: Family and Reform in the Old South.* New York: Oxford University Press, 1990.
An intellectual and social portrait of a key white supremacist, Edwin Ruffin, a self-made planter who too his own life in 1865 rather than face the Confederate defeat. As with many whites, Ruffin based his belief in the superiority of his race on science and the Bible. Science taught that the white race was superior to all colored races, and the Bible taught that God had created dark-skinned people to serve whites, as related in the story of Noah and his son Ham. 274 pages with maps, extensive notes, and an index.

Aptheker, Herbert. *Anti-Racism in U.S. History: The First Two Hundred Years.* New York: Greenwood Press, 1992.
Another interesting book by the Marxist historian on a subject not covered anywhere else. Anti-racists existed and more commonly among lower-class whites. Support for true equality appeared most visibly among white people who worked with blacks or lived close to them in towns and cities. This survey based on diaries, court records, and literature finds women to be more openly expressive of anti-racist ideas and values. It covers the period from the 1650's to the Civil War.

Bailey, David. *Shadow on the Church: Southwestern Evangelical Religion and the Issue of Slavery, 1783-1860.* Ithaca, N.Y.: Cornell University Press, 1985.

Southern religious denominations supported slavery, even those in Texas and Arkansas, the primary areas discussed in this book. Ministers preferred to ignore the issue, perhaps unable to deal with the topic in any thoughtful, decent way. An ugly, sad period for Christian churches, not one of which anywhere in the South, showed any support for abolition and an end to slavery. 293 pages with a selected bibliography and an index.

Binder, Frederick M. *The Color Problem in Early National America As Viewed by John Adams, Jefferson, and Jackson.* The Hague: Mouton, 1968.

The views of three presidents on slavery, equality, and Native Americans. None of these shapers of policy spoke in terms of economic, political, or social equality, although Adams and Jefferson were troubled by the concept of holding people in bondage. 177 pages with an index.

Burton, Orville Vernon, and Robert C. McMath, Jr., eds. *Class, Conflict, and Consensus: Antebellum Southern Community Studies.* Westport, Conn.: Greenwood Press, 1982.

Ten essays presented by historians at a Newberry Library Conference in 1978. In "Making Mississippi Safe for Slavery: The Insurrection Panic of 1835" (pages 96-127), Laurence Shore describes how fear brought out the worst aspects of white supremacy. Other contributions on religion, yeoman farmers, and attitudes toward slaves briefly address race relations and racism. 308 pages with twenty-seven tables, notes, and an index.

Campbell, Stanley W. *The Slave Catchers: Enforcement of the Fugitive Slave Law, 1850-1860.* Chapel Hill: University of North Carolina Press, 1968.

While most northerners opposed slave labor, only a few actively opposed enforcement of the 1850 Fugitive Slave Law. Federal marshals enforced the law and returned hundreds of runaways to their masters. Northern states passed "personal liberty" laws to protect fugitives but not one slave was prevented from being returned to the South by these laws. 236 pages with an appendix listing fugitive slave cases and an index.

Carpenter, Barbara, ed. *Ethnic Heritage in Mississippi.* Jackson: University Press of Mississippi, 1992.

Issued by the Mississippi Humanities Council, these essays cover Africans in colonial and territorial Mississippi, European colonization, discussions of Native American cultures from prehistoric times to the nineteenth century, and a photographic essay on "Ethnic Mississippi, 1992." 212 pages with an index.

Cecil-Fronsman, Bill. *Common Whites: Class and Culture in Antebellum North Carolina.* Lexington: University Press of Kentucky, 1992.

A reconstruction of the worldview of common whites, as told through their songs, stories, and other traditions. Begins with early colonial origins and goes to the end of the Civil War. Slavery was valued by even by those too poor to own slaves because it kept Africans from competing with whites for resources. Common whites made allies with the rich and race always appeared more important to them than social class. The lower middle class harbored the most racist attitudes. Unsure of their own value and worth as human beings, since most were very poor and unsuccessful, they clung to the myth of white supremacy which assured them that no matter how dumb and ignorant they might be they still belonged to a superior race of beings. 274 pages with an essay on sources, notes, and an index.

Clarke, Erskine. *Wrestlin' Jacob: A Portrait of Religion in the Old South.* Atlanta: John Knox Press, 1979.

Based on the career of Charles C. Jones, a white missionary to plantation slaves in Liberty County, Georgia, and Charleston, South Carolina. Jones taught blacks how to transcend and resist oppression in this world by keeping their eye on the next, and he promised them that God rewarded faithful servants. 207 pages with notes and an index.

Collins, Bruce. *White Society in the Antebellum South.* London: Longman, 1985.

A general survey with individual chapters on Indians, Africans, and their relations with whites. Why did ordinary southern whites get excited by the idea of slavery? Because it boosted their sense of pride and made their otherwise dreary lives livable. They were members of the "Great White Race." 216 pages with four maps and an index.

Craven, Wesley Frank. *White, Red, and Black: The Seventeenth-Century Virginian.* Charlottesville: University Press of Virginia, 1971.

Three long essays describing differences between African, European, and Native American cultures. Africans became slaves early through custom and usage, although slave laws did not appear until the 1650's. Indian population declined rapidly through contact with "white" diseases such as smallpox and influenza. They were not enslaved because they died too quickly. They also knew the country and could escape easily. White settlers came seeking adventure and wealth and had little concern for anything else. 114 pages with an index.

Degler, Carl N. *Place Over Time: The Continuity of Southern Distinctiveness.* Baton Rouge: Louisiana University Press, 1977.
The distinguished historians contributions to understanding racism and white society are many. This set of four essays finds racism and slavery central to shaping the South. Southerners used race, not economics, to defend the slave system. All whites gained something from the institution, either wealth or psychological satisfaction and most of the time both. 138 pages with an index.

Faust, Drew Gilpin, ed. *The Ideology of Slavery: Proslavery Thought in the Antebellum South, 1830-1860.* Baton Rouge: Louisiana State University Press, 1981.
The writings of seven proslavery spokesmen, including James Henry Hammond and George Fitzhugh, introduced by the editor and placed in their historical perspective. Shows the development of their thought and the critical ideas in defense of slavery and white supremacy. 306 pages with a selected bibliography and an index.

_____. *James Henry Hammond and the Old South: A Design for Mastery.* Baton Rouge: Louisiana University Press, 1982.
Examines how slave owners treated their slaves and the mentality that supported the institution of slavery. Hammond, a wealthy South Carolina planter, believed in the benevolence of human bondage. Slaves were his children, but they never returned his love. 407 pages with thirteen charts, two tables, illustrations, and an index.

_____. *A Sacred Circle: The Dilemma of the Intellectual in the Old South, 1840-1860.* Baltimore: The Johns Hopkins University Press, 1977.
A brief survey of the thought of novelist William Gilmore Simms, politician and planter James Henry Hammond, Edmund Ruffin, Professor Nathaniel Beverly Tucker, and George F. Holmes. All were southern thinkers who felt they were bringing the great truths of science, history, and religion to an unheeding world. Slavery was one of the truths and it placed a great burden on the slave owner, they had

to bring civilization and Christianity to a backward, savage race of people. 189 pages with notes and an index.

Ford, Lacy K., Jr. *Origins of Southern Radicalism: The South Carolina Upcountry, 1800-1860.* New York: Oxford University Press, 1988.
Why did the "fire-eaters," whites who would rather eat fire than give up on slavery, triumph among the larger number of whites who were not as dedicated to protecting unfree labor? Describes the circumstances and values of upcountry whites who found some security in dreams of racial supremacy. 414 pages with an index.

Franklin, John Hope. *The Militant South: 1800-1860.* Cambridge, Mass.: Harvard University Press, 1956.
A study of the leaders of the secession movement and their devotion to slavery and race, by the distinguished African American historian. The fundamental belief of the white supremacists was that all whites however wretched their lives belonged to a superior race. Perhaps the more wretched one's life the more fervently one needed this belief. 317 pages with an index.

_____. *A Southern Odyssey: Travellers in the Antebellum North.* Baton Rouge: Louisiana State University Press, 1976.
Details how a group of white southerners toured the North in the late 1850's trying to convince people to turn from free labor to slavery. Masters took good care of their slaves. Factory owners did nothing for their free laborers except pay them a meager salary. Slavery was by far the most productive, the most humanitarian, system of labor. 299 pages with a note on sources and an index.

Frederickson, George M. *The Black Image in the White Mind: The Debate on Afro-American Character and Destiny, 1817-1914.* New York: Harper & Row, 1971.
Studies the development of racist theory in science and politics. Racist ideology was central to American thought from the earliest debates over the nature of slavery to the end of World War I. Only then did liberal intellectual environmentalism challenge traditional thinking that asserted genetics controlled human destiny. Traditionalists asserted that human nature could not be changed, liberals believed that differences between individuals resulted from environmental factors, such as poverty and family life. Liberals believed prejudice could be eliminated through education. Scientific racism, its adherents believed, was grounded in the facts of nature, people were naturally unequal and

nothing could change that. 343 pages with extensive notes and an index.

_____. *White Supremacy: A Comparative Study in American and South African History.* New York: Oxford University Press, 1981.
A history of race relations in the United States and South Africa from 1619, the year the first Africans were brought to Jamestown, to the 1970's. Analyzes the attitudes of whites in both countries and how they have developed and supported racist policies. 356 pages with extensive notes and an index.

Freehling, William W. *Prelude to Civil War: The Nullification Controversy in South Carolina, 1816-1836.* New York: Harper & Row, 1965.
This first major crisis over dissolving the Union resulted not from a controversy over the tariff, but because of southern sensitivity over the slavery issue. South Carolina did try to nullify the tariff and asserted its right to decide which federal laws it would obey. Yet John C. Calhoun, author of the paper supporting nullification, was worried about slavery. If the federal government could make South Carolina obey a law its people opposed, then what would happen if Congress suddenly outlawed slavery? Would not slave states have to obey? Not if they accepted Calhoun's logic. 395 pages with an index.

Genovese, Eugene D. *The Slaveholders' Dilemma: Freedom and Progress in Southern Conservative Thought, 1820-1860.* Columbia: University of South Carolina Press, 1992.
Originally delivered as a lecture, Genovese's work provides an analysis of key southern intellectuals, including John C. Calhoun and Thomas Dew, and finds a searing critique of modern free market capitalism. The free market was the most dangerous destructive force in the modern world. Slavery meant order and stability, paternalism and responsibility. A society based on an absolute free market would destroy families, turn the poor into criminals, and allow many people to live in desperately impoverished circumstances, and no one would care. 116 pages with an index.

_____. *The World the Slaveholders Made: Two Essays in Interpretation.* New York: Pantheon Books, 1969.
Once slavery came into being, prejudice was quickly transformed into racism. Racism was an ideology of oppression and subordination that appealed to many non-slaveholders because of the security such feelings produced in otherwise meaningless and hopeless lives. 274 pages with an index.

Goldfield, David R. *Urban Growth in the Age of Sectionalism, 1847-1861.*
Baton Rouge: Louisiana State University Press, 1977.
Slave labor was essential to economic development in Virginia cities.
The slave codes used to control unfree labor became the Black Codes
in the aftermath of the Civil War. Whites preferred segregation as the
major form of race relations, first through slavery then through law.
Whites used laws to restrict African American mobility and to provide
a reliable supply of labor. 336 pages, fifty-seven tables, and an index.

Harris, J. William. *Plain Folk and Gentry in a Slave Society: White Liberty
and Black Slavery in Augusta's Hinterlands.* Middletown, Conn.:
Wesleyan University Press, 1985.
Another attempt to answer the question, Why did the vast majority of
non-slaveholding whites defend slavery? Only 25 percent of the residents of Augusta, Georgia, owned slaves, yet support for the system
was almost unanimous. Rich and poor alike shared a terrifying fear of
black people. Emancipation would mean race war and anarchy. Slaves
were contemptible beings who were savage and ignorant. The slave
system helped preserve order and protected society, especially white
women, from rape and ruin. 274 pages with twenty-nine tables, three
maps, illustrations, extensive notes, and an index.

Howard, Victor B. *Conscience and Slavery: The Evangelistic Calvinist
Domestic Missions, 1837-1861.* Kent, Ohio: Kent State University
Press, 1990.
A discussion of northern churches and their response to slavery. Some
did oppose slavery as a violation of individual liberty. Many denominations remained pro-slavery, including Presbyterians and Congrega-
tionalists, while others ignored the entire issue. 263 pages with notes,
a bibliography, and an index.

Inscoe, John C. *Mountain Masters: Slavery and the Sectional Crisis in
Western North Carolina.* Knoxville: University of Tennessee Press,
1989.
Proslavery ideology existed even in areas not dependent on slaves for
a labor force. The "Highlanders" of western North Carolina owned few
slaves, less than 10 percent of the population in this area was unfree.
Yet, whites were ready to fight and die for the Cause. Slavery became
a symbol for southern rights that were being trammelled upon by a
distant, alien government. The death of slavery would destroy white
freedom and lead to chaos and racial conflict. Thus, they fought. 348

pages with thirteen tables, seven maps, illustrations, a bibliography, and an index.

Kenzer, Robert. *Kinship and Neighborhood in a Southern Community: Orange County, North Carolina, 1841-1889.* Knoxville: University of Tennessee Press, 1987.
A brief discussion of slavery and race relations is included. An unusual work because it deals with people and relations before and after the Civil War. Generally, the freedmen's relations with their former masters was still based on subservience and inequality. As blacks gained more political rights because of the Fourteenth and Fifteenth Amendments whites reacted by segregating them into separate educational and public institutions. Race relations moved from slavery to segregation, which did exclude African Americans from equal participation in county government. 251 pages with twenty-four tables, illustrations, and an index.

Klein, Rachel N. *Unification of a Slave State: The Rise of the Planter Class in the South Carolina Backcountry, 1760-1808.* Chapel Hill: University of North Carolina Press, 1990.
Slaveholders did not trust small farmers without slaves, so they did not allow them to vote. The plantation masters maintained racial solidarity by promoting white supremacy and warning about the dangers of emancipation. White women would suffer horrible retribution at the hands of African savages. Slavery was necessary to protect the freedom and safety of all whites. As long as slave masters were in control, slaves would be in their proper place, just as a father made sure his children remained in their place. 331 pages with five maps, fifteen tables, and an index.

McCardell, John. *The Idea of a Southern Nation: Southern Nationalism and Southern Nationalists, 1830-1860.* New York: W. W. Norton, 1979.
Stresses the importance of race in the thinking of all white nationalists. Skin color distinguished superior from inferior races. The great Anglo-Saxon race had an important, God-given mission to perform, and white southerners had been chosen to make sure it was accomplished. The spread of Christianity and the preservation of civilized culture was the responsibility of the South. If the white race failed in this mission anarchy, chaos, and racial degradation would result. 394 pages with illustrations and an index.

McWhiney, Grady. *Cracker Culture: Celtic Ways in the Old South.* Tuscaloosa: University of Alabama Press, 1988.

Argues that southern culture is a variation of Celtic culture and is sharply different from the "English culture" of the Yankees. Celts, the ancestors of Scots, Welsh, and Irish, had strong beliefs in individualism, honor, and military virtues. Their racial views are only briefly described, and there is only a minimal discussion of slavery. 290 pages with notes and an index.

Nash, Gary B. *Red, White and Black: The Peoples of Early America.* Englewood Cliffs, N.J.: Prentice-Hall, 1974.
Still a useful textbook which serves as a starting point for the study of racial and cultural conflict in the United States. Provides information on Indians before Columbus, especially the Aztecs, down through the American Revolution. The introduction of slavery is described and the growth of slave society. Europeans made progress at a terrible cost in human suffering, enslavement, and degradation for others. 345 pages with a bibliography and an index.

Oakes, James. *The Ruling Race: A History of American Slaveholders.* New York: Alfred A. Knopf, 1982.
Challenges the Marxist view of slavery by stressing the capitalist ethic of slave owners. A portrait of the four hundred thousand slaveholders in the South from colonial times to the Civil War. Equality was inconceivable for the masters, who believed that blacks, as an inferior race, benefited greatly from slavery. Slavery also paid off by making huge amounts of money for cotton and rice growers. The white capitalists in the South had little trouble defending the right to own slaves, whatever made money in a free market economy was acceptable. In the eyes of the slaveholders, blacks could not handle freedom. They knew nothing of money, they were ignorant, and they were sexually promiscuous. Black slaves needed the protection of their white masters, and whites needed the protection of slavery. 307 pages with an index.

_____. *Slavery and Freedom: An Interpretation of the Old South.* New York: Alfred A. Knopf, 1990.
Slavery is defined as the denial of freedom. Southerners defined slavery as the denial of free market capitalism. They rejected modern liberal values such as equal opportunity and political equality. Southern slave owners defended their society by asserting the biological inferiority of the African Americans they held as slaves. They used this racism to build support even among white non-slaveholders. Racial slavery unified free society; the poorest white was equal to the richest. The

very idea of a "free" black was outrageous. A major interpretation of white racism, its causes, and its functions. The arguments advanced in this study represent a major change from those found in Oakes's earlier work, *The Ruling Race*, cited above. 246 pages with notes and an index.

Peterson, Thomas Virgil. *Ham and Japeth: The Mythic World of Whites in the Antebellum South.* Metuchen, N.J.: Scarecrow Press, 1978.
Examines white southern notions about the biblical legitimacy of slavery and racial superiority. The myth of Ham and Japeth, Noah's sons, gave religious authority to racism. Ham laughed at his father for being drunk and was sent away by God, who commanded Ham to be the servant of mankind forever. Ham's descendants—Africans—continue to bear that burden. Belief in this myth enabled whites to silence any challenge to their superiority by pointing to the hand of God as the creator of their superior position. Whites were the master race and the maker of the universe had deemed it so. Who could argue with that? 181 pages with extensive notes and an index.

Scarborough, William K. *The Overseer: Plantation Management in the Old South.* Baton Rouge: Louisiana State University Press, 1966.
Aimed at ascertaining the degree of competence which marked the general performance of the overseer class and to give them proper recognition for their contributions to economic growth. Most overseers were energetic, efficient, and competent. They viewed slaves with fear and condescension. An economic history of their role in the production process. 256 pages with nine tables, four charts, and an index.

Shore, Laurence. *Southern Capitalists: The Ideological Leadership of an Elite, 1832-1885.* Chapel Hill: University of North Carolina Press, 1986.
Because they were not so different from northern businessmen, members of the planter class could easily adopt the rhetoric and values of business culture after the Civil War. Their racism never lessened, and white supremacy remained a central theme of their culture. An analysis of the continuity of upper-class supremacist rhetoric and morality. 282 pages with notes, a bibliography, and an index.

Siegel, Frederick F. *The Roots of Southern Distinctiveness: Tobacco and Society in Danville, Virginia, 1780-1865.* Chapel Hill: University of North Carolina Press, 1987.
Describes a subregion that failed to develop economically. Its failures resulted not from values, farmers in the region enthusiastically subscribed to the spirit of capitalism, but from the economic structure of

tobacco production. The material conditions of the area, its climate, soil, and technical peculiarities, made life hard for all. Slavery had little significance here, but white farmers shared the racial views of their culture. 205 pages, with forty tables, three maps, a bibliography, notes, and an index.

Thornton, J. Mills, III. *Politics and Power in a Slave Society: Alabama, 1800-1860*. Baton Rouge: Louisiana State University Press, 1978.
A portrait of a political style and culture and how Alabamians viewed the frightening world. They were obsessed with the idea of slavery. Holding African Americans in bondage promoted feelings of equality and security among whites by dispensing with social classes among them. Without slavery and the doctrine of white supremacy, poor whites would be nothing but slaves themselves. 492 pages with three tables, illustrations, and an index.

Tise, Larry E. *Proslavery: A History of the Defense of Slavery in America, 1701-1840*. Athens: University of Georgia Press, 1987.
A study of the literature of white supremacy. The ideology of slavery expressed values held by most white Americans, north and south. There was a national acquiescence that slavery was morally acceptable. Had it not been for civil war that acceptance would not have been shattered. 501 pages with tables, illustrations, notes, a bibliography, and an index.

Toplin, Robert Brent. *Freedom and Prejudice: The Legacy of Slavery in the United States and Brazil*. Westport, Conn.: Greenwood Press, 1981.
A comparative study of tensions that arose out of the quest for emancipation in the nineteenth century. In both societies, there was a close connection between class inequality and race prejudice. Suggests that African Americans were seen as inferior even by abolitionists. 134 pages with notes, a bibliography, and an index.

Washington, Joseph R., Jr. *Anti-Blackness in English Religion, 1500-1800*. New York: The Edwin Mellen Press, 1984.
A massive study from its early roots in England to the anti-black attitudes of colonial American churches. Describes the symbolic and significant religious nature of anti-blackness. Traces the negative quality of the color black from Shakespeare to writers in revolutionary American newspapers. 603 pages with a bibliography, notes, and an index.

Wood, Forrest G. *The Arrogance of Faith: Christianity and Race in America from the Colonial Era to the Twentieth Century.* Boston: Northeastern University Press, 1990.

From the papal defense of inequality in 1510 to the ideas of 1920's white fundamentalism, Christianity played a crucial role in racist thought. It has been fundamentally racist in its ideology, organization, and practice. God mandated subservience on the part of Africans. Anti-black racism was so pervasive in America it infected every major religious denomination. 517 pages with notes, a bibliography, and an index.

Wyatt-Brown, Bertram. *Southern Honor: Ethics and Behavior in the Old South.* New York: Oxford University Press, 1982.

"Honor" was the fundamental value in white society. It meant white people's notions of right actions had to be enforced. It included the integrity of family life and the rule of men over women. Order and respectability had to be preserved. Public humiliation, shame, and disgrace were the most dishonorable things. Honor required a fight against evil, represented by black savagery. Violence, lynching, and killing were sometimes required to preserve honor. The omnipotent forces of evil had to be exterminated in bloody reprisal to uphold the values of the community. 597 pages with notes and an index. A 270-page abridged edition, *Honor and Violence in the Old South*, published by Oxford University Press in 1986, contains the essentials of the argument.

Chapter 6

RACE AND RECONSTRUCTION, 1865-1877

Alexander, Roberta Sue. *North Carolina Faces the Freedmen: Race Relations During Presidential Reconstruction, 1865-1867.* Durham, N.C.: Duke University Press, 1985.
Whites quickly set about establishing a system of race relations that kept blacks in a state of inferiority. Freedmen worked hard and peaceably, few committed crimes, but the majority of whites still believed chaos and economic disaster were just around the corner. Whites refused to believe they had lost the War and few were ready to view African Americans as equals. Nothing short of full-scale military occupation by Yankee troops and war-crimes trials for Confederate leaders would have led to any fundamental changes. The Civil War ended slavery but the struggle for equality had just begun. 238 pages with nine tables, notes, a bibliography, and an index.

Anderson, Eric, and Alfred A. Moss, Jr., eds. *The Facts of Reconstruction: Essays in Honor of John Hope Franklin.* Baton Rouge: Louisiana State University Press, 1991.
Nine essays by former students of John Hope Franklin and an afterword by the editors. Contains two especially interesting essays. In "Segregation and Reconstruction" (pages 79-99), Howard Rabinowitz asserts that segregation was always a customary practice in southern society, and often voluntarily adopted by the black community after the Civil War. The issue for African Americans became equal treatment within a segregated society, or "separate but equal" facilities. In "Counter Reconstruction: The Role of Violence in Southern Redemption" (pages 121-141), Michael Perman finds that violence and force were at the heart of the movement to restore white supremacy after the war. Beginning in Mississippi in 1874, where a black state representative was killed, whites organized into paramilitary bands and received active support from Democratic leaders as they attacked courthouses, jails, and government buildings in counties still controlled by Republicans. By 1877, this campaign of violence was successful and Reconstruction, the effort to gain equal rights for freedmen, was overthrown. 239 pages with an index.

Bentley, George R. *A History of the Freedmen's Bureau.* Philadelphia: University of Pennsylvania Press, 1955.

Methods used by the Freedmen's Bureau, an agency of the United States Army, helped African American freedmen through education, finding employment, offering legal protection, and establishing health care facilities. On the other hand, these efforts seriously hurt blacks by leading to increased racial hatred among whites. They simply could not abide the notion of the federal government helping a people they despised, feared, and had recently considered property. Help from Washington fed the flames of racial hostility in the South. 298 pages with notes and an index.

Berlin, Ira, et al., eds. *Freedom: A Documentary History of Emancipation, 1861-1867.* 4 vols. Cambridge, England: Cambridge University Press, 1985.

Volume 1, *The Destruction of Slavery*, has 331 documents arranged chronologically concerning slavery's demise in Virginia, North and South Carolina, Georgia, Florida, the District of Columbia, Louisiana, the Mississippi Valley, Maryland, Missouri, and Kentucky. Includes records from the Freedmen's Bureau, federal courts, the Army, Senate and House investigations, and the testimony and reactions of slaves, freedmen, slaveholders, and ordinary white southerners. Each chapter has an introductory essay and there is also a general introduction by Ira Berlin, the director of the Freedmen and Southern Society Project which collected these original sources. 852 pages with an index. Volume 2 documents *The Wartime Genesis of Free Labor: The Upper South* and volume 3 documents *The Wartime Genesis of Free Labor: The Lower South*, while volume 4 concerns *The Black Military Experience*.

_____, et al. *Slaves No More: Three Essays on Emancipation and the Civil War.* New York: Cambridge University Press, 1992.

Generated from the Freedmen and Southern Society Project, this work contains the introductory essays from the published volumes of documents: *The Destruction of Slavery*, *The Wartime Genesis of Free Labor: The Upper South*, *The Wartime Genesis of Free Labor: The Lower South*, and *The Black Military Experience*. 243 pages with an index.

Blassingame, John W. *Black New Orleans, 1860-1880.* Chicago: University of Chicago Press, 1973.

Chapter 7 discusses race relations. Black-white relations went back and forth between integration and segregation during Reconstruction. Blacks fought early attempts to establish segregation because they found it humiliating to use separate facilities such as streetcars. Segregation laws first established in 1867 were frequently violated. Integration existed in some schools and interracial marriage took place on occasion. Yet, segregation was the customary pattern in most areas of life. Blacks fought for equal treatment but whites wanted only total segregation, and by 1880 they had it. 301 pages with nineteen tables, illustrations, notes, a bibliography, and an index.

Carter, Dan T. *When the War Was Over: The Failure of Self-Reconstruction in the South, 1865-1867.* Baton Rouge: Louisiana State University Press, 1985.
Former Confederate leaders were racists, cautious and conservative, who wanted economic development. The represented the most constructive and creative response white southerners were able to make to their devastating defeat. They believed in paternalist race relations, blacks could be good children but could never be trusted on their own. Leaders shared the irrational fears of blacks savagery found among all whites. In race relations, their goal was to reintroduce slavery under a different name: legal segregation. 285 pages with an index.

Crouch, Barry A. *The Freedmen's Bureau and Black Texans.* Austin: University of Texas Press, 1992.
Bureau agents did what was humanly possible. They were dedicated, honest, and hardworking but their limited manpower could not prevent outbreaks of racial violence. Six blacks were murdered by a white mob after a riot in Brazos County, July 16, 1868. Such outbreaks became more frequent in the early 1870's. The Bureau could not handle these types of murders and could not accomplish its modest purpose of protecting the civil rights of freedmen because of an atmosphere of insurmountable racial hatred in the state. 187 pages with notes, an essay on sources, and an index.

Cruden, Robert. *The Negro in Reconstruction.* Englewood Cliffs, N.J.: Prentice-Hall, 1969.
A view of black-white relations after emancipation and the problems that arose when it became clear that freedom was not enough, that it also had to be accompanied by equality. White society was not yet ready to move in that direction. 182 pages with an index.

Current, Richard N. *Those Terrible Carpetbaggers.* New York: Oxford University Press, 1988.
A study of ten "carpetbaggers," northerners who went to live in the South after the Civil War and became involved in Republican politics. Dispels the myth that they exploited white southerners, were corrupt, and imposed capitalist values on the South. Facts reveal they were better educated, less corrupt, and more dedicated to community improvement than the average white southerner. They encouraged and supported political rights for blacks which earned them the utmost hatred of their "racial brothers." Most were out of power by 1874. 475 pages, with notes and an index.

Curry, Richard O., ed. *Radicalism, Racism, and Party Realignment: The Border States During Reconstruction.* Baltimore: The Johns Hopkins University Press, 1969.
Nine essays and an introduction on politics in Missouri, Kentucky, Tennessee, Maryland, West Virginia, and Delaware. Explores how the Democratic Party exploited white racial fears to regain power. Equal rights were not possible considering the intense racial hatred of whites toward African Americans. Border state politicians in the Democratic Party had no interest in enforcing the right to vote for blacks. By 1870, these states were all under the control of white racist regimes. The federal government did not intervene to protect the rights of freedmen. 331 pages with and index.

Drago, Edmund L. *Black Politicians and Reconstruction in Georgia: A Splendid Failure.* Baton Rouge: Louisiana State University Press, 1982.
In April, 1868, the Ku Klux Klan, through a campaign of violence, came close to taking control of the state. Federal military interference was minimal. Blacks played an important role in keeping the state Republican but then were betrayed by their own party. Fully 90 percent of the party's vote came from African Americans, but party control remained in the hands of whites. White Republicans did little for blacks, and voted with the Democratic minority in September, 1868, to expel all black members from the state legislature. The black political leadership in the state failed to organize resistance to this move. Dominated by ministers, their message after the expulsion was to accept reality, forgive, and accept all men as deserving of God's mercy. Not a message tending to elicit protest or even demands for equal rights. 201 pages with a bibliography and an index.

Duncan, Russell. *Entrepreneur for Equality: Governor Rufus Bullock, Commerce and Race in Post-Civil War Georgia.* Athens: University of Georgia Press, 1994.
Part carpetbagger and part scalawag, a white who supported black rights, Bullock became a symbol of "military-Negro-Yankee" oppression. He stood out to support equality, racial justice and one-man, one-vote. Impeached by the Georgia legislature for stealing money he lost his power. His alleged crime hardly mattered compared to the degradation of an entire people. White Georgians viewed things differently, however, and he was gone. 278 pages with a bibliography and an index.

_____. *Freedom's Shore: Tunis Campbell and the Georgia Freedmen.* Athens: University of Georgia Press, 1986.
Tunis Campbell was a black American who wanted to create a true color-blind democracy in McIntosh County, Georgia. He was also a Republican radical who created a political machine that maintained power four years longer than any other African American organization in the state. Deposed by the state legislature in 1876 for "corruption," he spent several years on a chain gang. Such was the fate of African Americans talking about equality in the post-Civil War south. 175 pages with notes and an index.

Engs, Robert F. *Freedom's First Generation: Black Hampton, Virginia, 1861-1870.* Philadelphia: University of Pennsylvania Press, 1979.
The development of Hampton Institute, the most influential educational institution for blacks in the late nineteenth century. Yet leaders of the school, mostly black, insisted on a demeaning role for their students. Only studies in agriculture and education were approved, no politics. Blacks were a majority in Hampton, a city of twenty thousand, and made great strides toward political equality. When whites became the majority group in 1890, however, they denied African Americans the right to hold office and supported taking away their right to vote. 236 pages with illustrations and an index.

Field, Phyllis F. *The Politics of Race in New York: The Struggle for Black Suffrage in the Civil War Era.* Ithaca, N.Y.: Cornell University Press, 1982.
A study of referenda in 1846, 1860, and 1869 concerning voting rights for blacks. White majorities rejected equal suffrage until 1869. Even after that vote narrowly granting the right to vote, blacks enjoyed few

changes in status in schools, housing, and employment opportunities. 264 pages with some statistical analysis and an index.

Fischer, Roger A. *The Segregation Struggle in Louisiana, 1862-1877.* Urbana: University of Illinois Press, 1974.
The attempt to end racial segregation in public schools and places of public accommodation—streetcars, theaters, and taverns—was unsuccessful. Segregation by law made an early appearance, and whites imposed it as soon as they returned to power. There never was a period when equal rights appeared possible. Segregation provided whites with a zone of security from what they saw as barbarism and criminality. 168 pages with an index.

Fitzgerald, Michael W. *The Union League Movement in the Deep South: Politics and Agricultural Change During Reconstruction.* Baton Rouge: Louisiana State University Press, 1989.
The Union League (also called the Loyal League), the first Radical Republican organization in the South, recruited thousands of African Americans to its cause, especially in Alabama and Mississippi. By 1869, however, the Ku Klux Klan had battered it into insignificance. It had supported voting rights and tenant farming for its members. 283 pages with a bibliography and an index.

Foner, Eric. *Reconstruction: America's Unfinished Revolution, 1863-1877.* New York: Harper & Row, 1988.
A major summary and evaluation of the problems, failures, and limited successes of the movement for political equality and economic reform. Racism contributed to the undoing of attempts to promote black civil and political rights. The disfranchisement of African American voters, beginning in many areas in 1868-1869 with the violent attacks by the Ku Klux Klan, enabled the victory of white supremacy to come very quickly. Most northerners had tired of the problems in the South and preferred to let the race question alone. 690 pages with maps, illustrations, a select bibliography, and an index.

Gerber, David A. *Black Ohio and the Color Line, 1860-1915.* Urbana: University of Illinois Press, 1976.
A study of patterns of race relations in a northern industrial state. Most blacks showed a great reluctance to challenge white supremacist views, at least in public. Blacks were not allowed full entrance into the mainstream of Ohio's business, political, or social community. They lost faith in the commitment of whites to full equality and favored,

instead, building a racial community. 500 pages with a map, a note on sources, and an index.

Gillette, William. *Retreat from Reconstruction: 1869-1879.* Baton Rouge: Louisiana University Press, 1979.
A study of presidential and congressional policies. The retreat from the goal of black political equality had several causes: waning of popular support among white northerners; the desire to get the nation back to normal after years of war; the reduction of federal troops in the South; the collapse of enforcement of voting rights, and the resurgence of racism in political campaigns North and South. Ideas of limited government and local control also crippled the effort. Equality seemed to mean that blacks had to take care of themselves. At a time when only strong action by the central government would protect black rights, conservatives in Congress and the press raised the issue of local autonomy and the "dangers" of central power. The government had to be restrained from imposing itself in local matters, such as race relations, rather than be trusted with the necessary power to do good. As a result of Reconstruction, peace reigned in the South after 1877, but there was no justice. 463 pages with notes, a bibliographical essay, and an index.

Holt, Thomas. *Black Over White: Negro Political Leadership in South Carolina During Reconstruction.* Urbana: University of Illinois Press, 1977.
Biographical data and detailed analysis of the black political leadership in South Carolina. Describes their social backgrounds and their political beliefs and accomplishments. Reconstruction was not a major success, but neither was it a total failure. One problem, black leaders were drawn largely from the free black community. As middle-class professionals who failed to act in or even understand the best interests of their largely peasant constituents, these leaders had no program or ideology beyond black unity. Neither did whites, of course, who maintained unity only through appeals to white supremacy. 269 pages with a bibliographical essay and an index.

Howard, Victor B. *Black Liberation in Kentucky: Emancipation and Freedom, 1862-1884.* Lexington: University Press of Kentucky, 1983.
Conservative Democrats gained control of the state, one of the four slave states to remain in the Union during the Civil War, as early as 1867. This meant that segregation began quickly and the Ku Klux Klan practically ran the state. Only the intervention of federal courts pre-

vented total exclusion of blacks from political society. Judges inter-
vened to protect education, the right of blacks to testify against whites
in trials, and the right to vote for freedmen. By 1880, even the courts
withdrew protection and blacks became fully second-class citizens.
222 pages with notes and an index.

Jaynes, Gerald David. *Branches Without Roots: Genesis of the Black
Working Class in the American South, 1862-1882.* New York: Oxford
University Press, 1986.
A chapter on "The Economic Origins of the Color Line" (pages
253-316) finds that southern white leaders moved from paternalistic
capitalism under slavery to segregated capitalism under free labor.
Racism was deeply imbedded in the minds of the South and the War
did not begin to erase it. In white-owned industries and factories, black
and white laborers would not be allowed to work together since it
would lead to violence. God ordained separation of the races and it
would always remain so. 351 pages with a statistical appendix and an
index.

Jones, Jacqueline. *Soldiers of Light and Love: Northern Teachers and
Georgia Blacks, 1865-1873.* Chapel Hill: University of North Carolina
Press, 1980. Reprint. Athens: University of Georgia Press, 1992.
The story of the women who volunteered to go south and teach the
freedmen in Freedmen's Bureau schools. Explores why they volunteered, how they lived and worked, what they accomplished, and what
they learned from their experience. 273 pages with an index.

Kennedy, Stetson. *After Appomattox: How the South Won the War.* Gainesville: University of Florida Press, 1995.
The essence of Reconstruction was the struggle between those who
wanted liberty and justice for all, and those who sought to maintain
white supremacy and oppression. The book's title indicates who won
in the view of this African American historian. Partially based on the
testimony of victims of Ku Klux Klan violence before a Joint Congressional Committee established in 1872. Violence ended the struggle for
equal rights. 321 pages with illustrations, a bibliography, and an index.

Kolchin, Peter. *First Freedom: The Responses of Alabama's Blacks to
Emancipation and Reconstruction.* Westport, Conn.: Greenwood
Press, 1972.
Freedmen wanted to be as free as possible and insisted on behaving
independently. They wanted wages or land or education or the ability
to move from place to place at their own whim. From their own point

of view, even sharecropping and tenant farming were vastly better than slavery. They refused to conform to the image of slaves: docile, helpless, and ignorant, and demanded the right to think for themselves. 215 pages with seventeen tables, three maps, notes, and an index.

Litwack, Leon F. *Been in the Storm So Long: The Aftermath of Slavery.* New York: Alfred A. Knopf, 1979.

A major interpretation drawing on Federal Writers' Project interviews done with former slaves in the 1930's, and also material from the Freedmen's Bureau and other sources from the 1860's. Describes "the feel of freedom" for people who never experienced it before. Discusses songs, hymns, folklore, and other oral traditions. Describes the terror of Ku Klux Klan attacks and the fears and despair, plus a few victories, of the freedmen. Great emphasis is placed on the importance of religion and the first involvement in voting and politics. Sharecropping emerged to replace slavery as a means of employment but for many blacks it was a great step forward. Being tied to the land and working for a landlord was better than slavery, because blacks were allowed to make at least some key decisions for themselves. 651 pages with a select bibliography, notes, and an index.

McPherson, James M. *The Struggle for Equality: Abolitionists and the Negro in Civil War and Reconstruction.* Princeton, N.J.: Princeton University Press, 1964.

Abolitionists, such as William Lloyd Garrison, who had supported an immediate end to slavery since the 1820's, showed a greater concern for the difficulties of race relations in the South than any other Americans, except blacks themselves. They battled for voting rights and civil rights in Congress, and Garrison became active in the movement to educate the freed slaves. He denounced racial discrimination and prejudice. Abolitionists shared fully in the black struggle for equality recognizing that freedom was not enough. 474 pages with notes, a bibliographical essay, and an index.

Magdol, Edward. *A Right to the Land: Essays on the Freedmen's Community.* Westport, Conn.: Greenwood Press, 1977.

A description of the activities of the Freedmen's Bureau from the point of view of African American former slaves. Includes a discussion of land policy, the needs of the freedmen, and what they expected from bureau agents. 290 pages with tables, illustrations, and a index.

Morgan, Lynda J. *Emancipation in Virginia's Tobacco Belt, 1850-1870.* Athens: University of Georgia Press, 1992.

A study of free blacks, slaves, and freedmen. Describes the transition from slavery to freedom and the emergence of an African-Virginian community. Stresses economic changes in the tobacco belt and how the decline of the industry influenced freedom, family, religion, class, and politics. Segregation seemed to emerge early; freedmen were treated just the way free blacks had been treated. 329 pages with a map, a bibliography, notes, and an index.

Nieman, Donald G., ed. *From Slavery to Sharecropping: White Land and Black Labor in the Rural South, 1865-1900.* New York: Garland, 1994.
Twenty essays by historians introduced by the editor. Former slaves preferred sharecropping to the wage system because it gave them greater independence, no white man constantly stared over their shoulder. Still, the freed slaves led lives of grinding poverty. Many saved what they could, however, and managed to buy land. By 1880, about 20 percent of black farmers owned some land. Even such small plots of land symbolized freedom, and former slaves sacrificed much to gain possession of it. See especially James Smallwood's "Perpetuation of Caste: Black Agricultural Workers in Reconstruction" (pages 227-246) for the problems of land ownership. 415 pages.

_____. *To Set the Law in Motion: The Freedmen's Bureau and the Legal Rights of Blacks, 1865-1868.* Millwood, N.Y.: KTO Press, 1979.
A collection of essays including two on slavery and emancipation: Philip Shaw Paludan's "Hercules Unbound: Lincoln, Slavery, and the Intentions of the Framers" (pages 1-22), and Paul Finkelstein's "The South Bend Fugitive Slave Case and the Value of 'Justice Delayed'" (pages 23-51). 197 pages with an index.

Novak, Daniel A. *The Wheel of Servitude: Black Forced Labor After Slavery.* Lexington: University Press of Kentucky, 1978.
A brief study of how laws were used to legally reenslave freed blacks. Focused on Kentucky and its Black Codes, it describes how peonage (or debt slavery), agricultural contract labor for prisoners, and vagrancy laws were used to reimpose unfree labor in the late 1860's. Similar methods of legalizing slavery emerged throughout the South. 126 pages with an index.

Oubre, Claude F. *Forty Acres and a Mule: The Freedmen's Bureau and Black Ownership.* Baton Rouge: Louisiana State University Press, 1978.
In July, 1866, Congress passed the Southern Homestead Act. It promised much but failed to provide the needs of most freed slaves. They

had until January 1, 1867, to enter land confiscated from disloyal whites and claim it as their own. No further assistance, no mule contrary to legend, was provided. The sixty-five hundred former slaves who took up this offer found the land of poor quality, most of it woods, swamp, or totally treeless. Fewer than one thousand stayed the five years required to gain full title to the land. 212 pages with an index.

Perman, Michael. *Emancipation and Reconstruction, 1862-1879.* Arlington Heights, Ill.: Harlan Davidson, 1987.
A brief survey summarizing recent interpretations of this key period in America history and race relations. The central question is not why Reconstruction failed to create political equality but whether it had any chance of succeeding in the first place. The problems involved were so complex, such as the whole question of promoting any idea of equality to white southerners, they were virtually incapable of solution. In later work (see his essay in *The Facts of Reconstruction*, edited by Eric Anderson and cited above), Perman places much more emphasis on violence as the major reason for the failure of the post-Civil War effort to promote political equality. 150 pages with a bibliographical essay and an index.

_____. *Reunion Without Compromise: The South and Reconstruction, 1865-1868.* Cambridge, England: Cambridge University Press, 1973.
The reactions and attitudes of southern white political politicians and the power of race in the white mind. Portrays the great bitterness and hostility felt by former Confederates toward the North and its attempt to promote political equality. Shows the difficulties involved in dealing with white supremacists. The South would never surrender its racial patterns and beliefs.

_____. *The Road to Redemption: Southern Politics, 1869-1879.* Chapel Hill: University of North Carolina Press, 1984.
Shows how a coordinated campaign of physical and psychological intimidation overthrew Reconstruction. White "Redeemers" used violent and illegal means to gain legitimate power. Violence preceded every election, although Democratic Party leaders usually called it off a few weeks before voting, lest it attract the attention of federal authorities. Race, in the form of white calls for unity, was the dominant issue in every campaign. 376 pages wit an index.

Rabinowitz, Howard N. *The First New South: 1865-1920.* Arlington Heights, Ill.: Harlan Davidson, 1992.

A brief survey of political and social history. Includes discussions of race relations, disfranchisement, Populism, and the Progressive Era. Loss of voting rights for blacks became almost total by 1898. After Louisiana imposed rigid new registration requirements, including a "literacy test," black registration fell from 95.6 percent of eligible males to 9.5 percent. White voters always found race a more important issue than social class. All whites preferred segregation, and blacks had little voice in the matter. 232 pages with an index.

_____, ed. *Southern Black Leaders of the Reconstruction Era.* Urbana: University of Illinois Press, 1982.
Fourteen essays by historians on African American congressmen, senators, state, and local leaders. Aimed at clearing up distortions given in negative portraits drawn by an earlier generation of pro-white historians. Provides information on issues, elections, charges of corruption, and how they lost or were driven from power. 422 pages with fifteen illustrations and an index.

Rable, George C. *But There Was No Peace: The Role of Violence in the Politics of Reconstruction.* Athens: University of Georgia Press, 1984.
A study of the political, social, economic, and psychological divisions in the South and of the political and racial warfare that finally led to the collapse of Reconstruction. Describes the Ku Klux Klan's role in helping bring down Republican governments in Georgia, Louisiana, Mississippi, and other states. A paralyzing sense of fear gripped southerners in the 1870's brought about by the Klan and the failure of any authorities to assert control and order. 257 pages with a bibliographical essay, notes, and an index.

Richardson, Joe M. *The Negro in the Reconstruction of Florida, 1865-1877.* Tallahassee: University of Florida Press, 1965.
Richardson finds that racial segregation appeared quickly after the demise of slavery. He challenges the view that there was a period of time after the Civil War when race relations were relatively friendly and peaceful.

Roark, James L. *Masters Without Slaves: Southern Planters in the Civil War and Reconstruction.* New York: W. W. Norton, 1977.
Traces the impact of secession, war, defeat, and the movement for equality upon the beliefs of the white ruling class as seen in diaries and other primary sources left by the forty-three thousand planters who made up this class in 1860. After the war, restoration of racial control became their most important requirement. Otherwise, "Negro crimi-

nals," poor whites, and scalawags (the few white southerners who supported equal rights), might take over. 273 pages with notes and an index.

Rose, Willie Lee. *Rehearsal for Reconstruction: The Port Royal Experiment.* New York: Bobbs-Merrill, 1964.
The island off the coast of South Carolina was abandoned by whites in November, 1861, leaving behind ten thousand slaves. Early the next year, fifty-three northern missionaries, most of them abolitionists, came in and began an experiment in education and equality. Port Royal became a proving ground for freed slaves and they were given land and equipment to begin farms. This model was supposed to be followed by the Freedmen's Bureau when the war was over, but it was not. 442 pages with an index.

Sawrey, Robert D. *Dubious Victory: The Reconstruction Debate in Ohio.* Lexington: University Press of Kentucky, 1992.
A study of racial attitudes and politics in a key northern state. Racial prejudice keyed the Republican defeat in 1867 state elections as the Democrats used racism to unify their white support. Republicans would bring blacks into they state, they charged. An amendment that would have given blacks the right to vote failed and political equality for blacks was denied. 194 pages with illustrations, a select bibliography, notes, and an index.

Shofner, Jerrell H. *Nor Is It Over Yet: Florida in the Era of Reconstruction, 1863-1877.* Gainesville: Florida State University Press, 1974.
White racism carried over from slavery into Black Codes and Jim Crow legislation. There was no period of interracial cooperation and politics as white supremacy dominated Democratic Party ideology.

Smallwood, James M. *Time of Hope, Time of Despair: Black Texans During Reconstruction.* Port Washington, N.Y.: Kennikat Press, 1981.
Sees segregation emerging quickly after the demise of slavery based on prior treatment of free blacks. Four hundred free blacks lived in the state before the Civil War, but they were treated little better than slaves and had to obey laws governing slaves. From 1865 to 1877, any assertion of equality by African Americans met with terrorism and violence. The United States Army and other federal authorities did little to stop it. White supremacists had returned to power by 1873. 202 pages with notes and an index.

Trelease, Allen W. *Reconstruction: The Great Experiment.* New York: Harper & Row, 1971.
A major study of how violence and terrorism brought about the overthrow of any movement toward equal rights in the aftermath of the Civil War. Includes a bibliography and an index.

_____. *White Terrorism: The Ku Klux Klan Conspiracy and Southern Reconstruction.* New York: Harper & Row, 1972.
A terrorist group aimed at preserving white supremacy, the Ku Klux Klan used violence to win back white control of the South. Terrorism was the quickest road to victory and Klan inspired beatings, whippings, and lynchings cast fear into the hearts of all freed slaves. The Klan's most important effect was to show that Republican governments, which had supported equal rights, could not control terror. Without federal assistance and a large-scale military occupation local governments were powerless to cope with the violence. 557 pages with illustrations and an index.

Vincent, Charles. *Black Legislators in Louisiana During Reconstruction.* Baton Rouge: Louisiana State University Press, 1976.
Blacks constituted 50.1 percent of Louisiana's population in 1870, but they never had a majority in the legislature. From 1868 to 1877, there were twenty-four state senators and ninety-nine representatives. Contrary to the still-popular notion that "Negro-dominated" Republican governments stole the state and the South blind, these legislators, mostly from the free black community, did not attempt to pass vindictive laws against whites. Instead, they worked for universal education for all, supported separate schools for blacks, and put more money into prison reform and mental hospitals. They put party loyalty ahead of race. Whites still hated and feared them and recaptured the state by 1877 after a campaign of violence. 262 pages with an index.

Wilson, Theodore Brantner. *The Black Codes of the South.* University: University of Alabama Press, 1965.
Describes the discriminatory effects of the racial laws passed by white governments in the South in 1865. The laws were aimed at maintaining a system of economic exploitation while granting a minimum level of freedom. 177 pages with a bibliography.

Woodward, C. Vann. *The Strange Career of Jim Crow.* New York: Harper & Row, 1955.
Revised several times, this classic interpretation aims to show segregation was not a longstanding southern tradition but a recent develop-

ment in response to changing political conditions. Woodward argues that segregation did not appear until the post-1890 period in an attempt by white rulers to prevent any possible cooperation between blacks and poor whites, as the Populists were calling for. Such a coming together of the lower class might have given it a majority of voters and could have led to radical economic reforms. Appeals to white supremacy prevent the birth of an interracial coalition of the poor. Most studies reject this analysis and see a long history of segregation, racism, and oppression.

Chapter 7

RACE, RIOTS, AND LYNCHING

Allen, Robert L. *The Port Chicago Mutiny: The Story of the Largest Mass Mutiny Trial in United States Naval History.* New York: Amistad Press, 1993.

On July 17, 1944, an explosion at a Navy ammunition base near San Francisco killed 320 sailors, 202 of whom were black. This incident occurred at a time when most African Americans in the Navy could do little more than load ships because of open prejudice and accusations that they were not intelligent or brave enough for any other role. A few weeks after the accident, 258 survivors, all of whom were black, refused to work on another ship unless more adequate safety provisions were adopted. All of them were court-martialled and received prison sentences of between eight and fifteen years. The author is a son of one of the survivors. 192 pages with an index.

Ayers, Edward L. *Vengeance and Justice: Crime and Punishment in the Nineteenth Century American South.* New York: Oxford University Press, 1984.

Examines the cultural and structural components of crime and punishment from about 1800 to 1900. Violence was a product of poverty, lack of education, and a strict construction of a "code of honor." In the South, among both blacks and whites, violence became associated with manhood. Honor meant an acute sensitivity to insults. For white males protecting women, the most important symbol of white supremacy, lynching became the most important means of maintaining purity, honor, and superiority. From 1889 to 1893, more than seven hundred lynchings took place in the South, the bloodiest period in the history of lynching. Burning rapists was like burning witches; people knew what they were doing. The were ridding the community of a terrible and elusive foe even if the victim was totally innocent. 353 pages with extensive notes and an index.

Baiamonte, John V., Jr. *Spirit of Vengeance: Nativism and Louisiana Justice, 1921-1924.* Baton Rouge: Louisiana State University Press, 1986.

This work focuses on anti-Italian violence in New Orleans and covers the trial and "judicial lynching" of six Italian immigrants accused of killing a bank guard. All six were hanged on very flimsy evidence. Italians were often seen as part of the "colored races" in many southern states and suffered the subsequent discrimination. 257 pages with illustrations and an index.

Bass, Jack, and Jack Nelson. *The Orangeburg Massacre.* Atlanta: Mercer University Press, 1984.
The story of a bloodbath that occurred on February 8, 1968, in Orangeburg, South Carolina. Three black students, part of a group protesting exclusion from a bowling alley, were shot by the police. After a brief trial a jury found the policemen innocent of all charges. The jury said they acted in self-defense and that the real perpetrators of any crime were "outside agitators" stirring up the black community. Two reporters who covered the story explore the case in depth by talking to both sides in the tragedy. A police coverup took place and the officers guilty of murder walked free. 244 pages with an index.

Benjamin, Gerald. *Race Relations and the New York City Commission on Human Rights.* Ithaca, N.Y.: Cornell University Press, 1972.
Examines the circumstances leading to the Harlem Riots of August 1, 1943. A police shooting started it, as was true of so many post-1940 riots. Discusses the city's response to the violence and the establishment of the Commission on Human Rights. Officials tried to adopt new approaches to race relations after the riot but seldom had any idea of how difficult it would be to change attitudes and perceptions of the police and the public. 274 pages with an index.

Berry, Mary Frances. *Black Resistance/White Law: A History of Constitutional Racism in America.* New York: Penguin Press, 1994.
Originally published in 1971 by Berry, a noted scholar who was appointed to serve on the United States Civil Rights Commission by President Clinton in 1993, this work includes discussions of lynchings, riots, and "racial murders." Concludes that the national government has used the constitution, since 1787, to maintain the racial status quo. Civil rights laws have reflected the will of whites to keep African Americans "permanent mudsills." Whites have always treated blacks more violently than other minorities and have received less legal protection. 319 pages with a bibliographical note and an index.

Bruce, Dickson D., Jr. *Violence and Culture in the Antebellum South.* Austin: University of Texas Press, 1979.
Whites in the pre-Civil War South accepted violence as a necessary force in society. It improved the social health by eliminating the weak

and the "criminal class." All classes, planters, middle- and lower-class whites, slaves, and free blacks supported brutality. Violence was part of human nature. It could not be transcended. Men were weak and corruptible and the possibilities of a peaceful, happy life were quite limited. Greed, envy, and malice ruled. Violence, whether dueling, fighting, murdering, or lynching, was the best way to protect yourself and your family from the forces of evil in the world. Individuals had to be ready to kill or be killed. 322 pages with an index.

Brundage, W. Fitzhugh. *Lynching in the New South: Georgia and Virginia, 1880-1930.* Urbana: University of Illinois Press, 1993.
A comparison of two states: Georgia, which experienced the most racial violence of all southern states, and Virginia, which had relatively little. Lynching was only one method used by whites to defend white supremacy. More than 85 percent of the more than five thousand victims in the period described were black and most stood accused of violating the unwritten code "protecting" white women. Lynchings declined in the 1930's, although 1953 was the first year the United States did not record a single lynching. One suggested reason, the number of legal executions began to rise during the same time. The state took the place of the mob as chief executioner. An appendix lists all victims in the two states, the date of the lynching, and the alleged crime of the victim. 375 pages with extensive notes and an index.

Carter, Dan T. *Scottsboro: A Tragedy of the American South.* Baton Rouge: Louisiana State University Press, 1969. Reprint. New York: Oxford University Press, 1971.
Describes one of the worst tragedies in modern legal history—a case in which the nine defendants suffered horribly for a crime that they never committed. The case did, however, lead to a Supreme Court decision requiring an attorney for defendants in death penalty cases. In another decision involving this case, the Court also called for an end to all-white juries. 314 pages, illustrations, and an index.

Cortner, Richard C. *A Mob Intent on Death: The NAACP and the Arkansas Riot Cases.* Middletown, Conn.: Wesleyan University Press, 1988.
The story of *Moore v. Dempsey* (1923), a landmark Supreme Court decision concerning the right of "due process." Ten people had been killed in October of 1919 during interracial fighting in Phillips County, Arkansas. Sixty-seven blacks received prison sentences and twelve others were condemned to death by white juries in the aftermath. The rioting began when police broke up a meeting of the Progressive

Farmers Union, an interracial organization. Several black members were killed, but no one was ever charged in those deaths. The NAACP became involved and convinced the United States Supreme Court that the African Americans had not received fair and impartial trials. Two years later all prisoners, including those sentenced to death, had been released. 241 pages with notes, illustrations, and an index.

_____. *A "Scottsboro" Case in Mississippi: The Supreme Court and Brown v. Mississippi* Jackson: University Press of Mississippi, 1986.
A key case from 1936 defining the rights of defendants under "due process." The United States Supreme Court reversed the convictions of three black tenant farmers sentenced to death for a murder. The case began with the killing of a white planter in 1934. Police arrested three African Americans and tortured them until they confessed. Within one week, an all-white jury convicted them and sentenced them to hanging. The NAACP took up an appeal and convinced a unanimous Court that "coerced confessions" denied defendants of due process. All three were released. 174 pages with notes and an index.

Downey, Dennis B., and Raymond M. Hyser. *No Crooked Death: Coatesville, Pennsylvania, and the Lynching of Zachariah Walker.* Urbana: University of Illinois Press, 1991.
One of the few studies of a lynching in a northern state. A white mob burned Walker alive in August 13, 1911, one of seventy such crimes in the United States that year. The victim had while drunk fired shots at two Polish steelworkers and then killed a policemen trying to arrest him. A mob dragged Walker from his hospital bed, beat him severely, and then set him afire. An all-white jury acquitted the lynchers. 174 pages with a bibliographical essay and an index.

Egerton, John. *Shades of Gray: Dispatches from the Modern South.* Baton Rouge: Louisiana State University Press, 1991.
Thirteen essays by a journalist and historian, including "Maurice Mays and the Knoxville Race Riot of 1919" (pages 164-188). After a white woman had been shot and killed in her home, a white mob invaded a black neighborhood, smashing windows, shooting into houses, and beating pedestrians. Two blacks were reported killed by the police, though in reality the number of dead might have reached thirty. Police arrested Maurice Mays, a popular black leader, for the murder and he was eventually executed, although totally innocent according to later evidence. 268 pages with an index.

Ellsworth, Scott. *Death in a Promised Land: The Tulsa Race Riot of 1921.*
Baton Rouge: Louisiana University Press, 1982.
Chronicles a riot on May 31-June 1, 1921, leading to perhaps more
than 250 deaths, even though only twenty-seven were officially recorded. A white mob attacked the black community of Greenwood,
Tulsa's black district, after a black man allegedly made improper
advances toward a white girl. The incident took place on a elevator in
downtown Tulsa when Dick Rowland, a bootblack, accidently stepped
on the operator's foot. She screamed, charged that she had been
assaulted, and one newspaper even claimed she had been raped. Police
arrested Rowland and a mob followed him to the police station. After
several hours of shouting for justice shots rang out and whites raced to
the black neighborhood. The mob killed dozens of residents and burned
and destroyed more than one thousand homes and businesses. Several
weeks later a jury later found Rowland not guilty of charges of assault.
No charges were brought against any member of the mob. 159 pages
with photographs taken during the riot, maps, a foreword by John Hope
Franklin, and an index.

Friedman, Lawrence J. *The White Savage: Racial Fantasies in the Post-
bellum South.* Englewood Cliffs, N.J.: Prentice-Hall, 1970.
A study of white hate and why the killing and maiming of black people
has been so essential to the white south and its culture. Explores why
white Americans, north and south, have spent so much time and energy
hating black Americans. Discusses the period from 1865 to the end of
World War I, paying special attention to popular culture including early
films such as *Birth of a Nation*, which was the ultimate white racist
film. According to Friedman, there was never a time when whites and
blacks got along well. 184 pages with an index.

Grimshaw, Allen D., ed. *Racial Violence in the United States.* Chicago:
Aldine Publishing, 1969.
Compiled by a sociologist, this work is a massive collection of journalistic, historical, and sociological views of racial violence in America
from colonial times to the 1960's. Essays on slave revolts, the Ku Klux
Klan, and twentieth century race riots. Almost every incident to rioting
is covered, including "What Happened at Columbia, Tennessee, February 25, 1946." There, two blacks were killed after a black man said
something to a white woman in a store. Whites proceeded to burn down
parts of the black community and rioted until the National Guard
restored order. The incident is representative of a typical riot in a typical
small southern town. 553 pages with an index.

Hair, William Ivy. *Carnival of Fury: Robert Charles and the New Orleans Race Riot of 1900.* Baton Rouge: Louisiana State University Press, 1976.

From July 25 to July 27, 1900, Robert Charles, a black laborer, shot and killed twenty-seven whites, including seven policemen. This biography of Charles follows his life from childhood in rural Mississippi to his death at age thirty-four at the hands of New Orleans police. His death set off a riot as a white mob beat three blacks to death and injured fifty-six more. Charles had been a black nationalist follower of Bishop Henry Turner before he started killing. 216 pages with illustrations, a bibliography, and an index.

Hall, Jacquelyn Dowd. *Revolt Against Chivalry: Jessie Daniel Ames and the Women's Campaign Against Lynching.* Rev. ed. New York: Columbia University Press, 1993.

Originally published in 1983, this edition includes a new introduction discussing the Anita Hill-Clarence Thomas hearings, in which Justice Thomas made a highly publicized comment comparing his case to those of blacks who were tortured and lynched. A few white women did fight lynching beginning in the 1920's, although they were condemned as traitors to the South and to their race. The racism that caused whites to murder blacks cannot be understood apart from their sexism. 405 pages with a select bibliography and an index.

Howard, Gene L. *Death at Cross Plains: An Alabama Reconstruction Tragedy.* University: University of Alabama Press, 1984.

The story of a mass lynching on July 11, 1870. The Ku Klux Klan executed five black men for "talking the wrong way" to white people. A white Canadian minister was also hanged for talking to blacks. The killers were all men of distinction from Cross Plains, a small community in north Alabama and no one was ever punished. 151 pages with notes and an index

Howard, Walter T. *Extralegal Violence in Florida During the 1930's.* London: Susquehanna University Press, 1995.

A detailed description of fifteen lynchings during the Depression, the most in any state in the 1930's. Evidence strongly suggests that blacks were lynched by whites to maintain social dominance. An African American historian provides a bloody, angry portrait of mob violence and intense racial hatred. 207 pages with notes and a short bibliography.

Ingalls, Robert P. *Urban Vigilantes in the New South: Tampa, 1882-1936.*
Knoxville: University of Tennessee Press, 1988.
Descriptions of lynchings, floggings, tar-and-featherings, and terrorist
attacks against "agitators," usually union organizers. Tampa gained a
reputation as one of the "worst centers of repression" in the United
States during the 1920's and 1930's. Violence became an accepted form
of community justice for white citizens. Violence was used to protect
the existing racial and economic order. 286 pages with illustrations,
maps, a bibliography, and an index.

McGovern, James R. *Anatomy of a Lynching: The Killing of Claude Neal.*
Baton Rouge: Louisiana State University Press, 1982.
A brief analysis and description of one of the most violent and brutal
murders in American history. A Florida mob tortured, mutilated, and
lynched Claude Neal in 1934 and then burned down much of the
community in which he lived. Neal was alleged to have had sexual
relations with a white girl, thus violating a serious taboo. Based on
interviews with African Americans in Greenwood, Florida, scene of
most of the horror. Many still demanded anonymity because of continuing fear of white retaliation. 170 pages with notes and an index.

Platt, Anthony, ed. *The Politics of Riot Commissions: A Collection of
Official Reports and Critical Essays.* New York: Macmillan, 1971.
Selections from newspapers, government investigations and reports,
and eyewitness accounts. Includes documents on riots in East St. Louis
in 1917, Chicago in 1919, New York in 1935, Detroit in 1943, Los
Angeles (Watts) in 1965, and various cities in the United States from
1967 to 1970. A useful collection of hard-to-find sources. 534 pages
with notes and an index.

Prather, H. Leon, Sr. *We Have Taken a City: Wilmington Racial Massacre
and Coup of 1898.* Rutherford, N.J.: Farleigh Dickinson University
Press, 1984.
A African American historian writes about one of the most horrible
racial disturbances of the Progressive Era. Wilmington, North Carolina, erupted in racial fury when armed white Democrats marched on
city hall and drove a recently elected Republican government from
power. Fourteen people died in six hours of brutal beatings and burn-
ings. 214 pages with notes, a bibliographical essay, and an index.

Rudwick, Elliott. *Race Riot at East Saint Louis, July 2, 1917.* New York,
Athenaeum, 1972.

An account of a riot leading to the deaths of thirty-nine African Americans and nine whites. Whites mobs set upon black soldiers being trained at a nearby base, after rumors of soldiers talking to white women spread. One of the most brutal riots on record with bodies being hung from lampposts and many mutilations taking place. Puts the riot into the larger context of northern race relations during the World War I era. 300 pages with notes, illustrations, tables, and an index.

Shapiro, Herbert. *White Violence and Black Response: From Reconstruction to Montgomery.* Amherst: University of Massachusetts Press, 1988.
A extensive and detailed survey of the causes and effects of racial violence. Concludes that millions of African Americans have lived in fear of great brutality and that all have suffered great harm because of the cultural stresses brought about by white racism. 565 pages with notes, illustrations, and an index.

Singer, Benjamin D., and Richard W. Osborn. *Black Rioters: A Study of Social Factors and Communication in the Detroit Riot.* Lexington, Mass.: D. C. Heath, 1970.
A study of the 1967 riots. Black participants tended to be less educated, had lower incomes, and lower occupational status than non-rioters. They were isolated from active participation in Detroit's economic and political system by racism and hostility. The government and police were never responsive to them and they felt great hostility toward white society in general. 180 pages with charts, tables, and an index.

Smead, Howard. *Blood Justice: The Lynching of Mack Charles Parker.* New York: Oxford University Press, 1986.
A case study of one of the last lynchings in the United States, 1959 in Poplarville, Mississippi. It involved charges of interracial rape and then a premeditated vigilante-style murder. None of the lynchers received any punishment, although most were known and identified. Lynching disappeared in the South after this tragedy because whites were less likely to get away with it. The FBI, the major northern newspapers and television networks, and even a few state government leaders became involved in publicizing these types of crimes. 248 pages with notes, a bibliography, and an index.

Tolnay, Stewart E., and E. M. Beck. *A Festival of Violence: An Analysis of Southern Lynchings, 1882-1930.* Urbana: University of Illinois Press, 1995.

A study of the 2,805 lynchings that took place in ten southern states from 1882 to 1930. That represented an average of one lynching a week, every week for forty-eight years. Among lynching victims, 94 percent were black men who died at the hands of white mobs. Not a single member of a lynch mob was ever punished for participating in that crime. Lynchings, however, were only part of the problem. Beatings, whippings, riots, and threats of violence also had to be faced daily by African Americans. Lynching was used to maintain the race lines in the South and to uphold the racial supremacy of poor whites. 297 pages with notes, maps, illustrations, charts, graphs, references, and an index.

Tuttle, William M., Jr. *Race Riot: Chicago in the Red Summer of 1919.* New York: Atheneum, 1975.
Describes the origins and consequences of a riot that led to more than forty deaths. The riot was born in the attitudes of racial superiority held by the white majority. An excellent study based on government records, newspaper files, eyewitness accounts, a testimony from police records. 305 pages with photographs, maps, notes, and an index.

Vandal, Gilles. *The New Orleans Riot of 1866: Anatomy of a Tragedy.* Lafayette: University of Southwestern Louisiana Press, 1983.
A three-hour riot in July that left fifty people dead and almost three hundred wounded. It followed riots in Memphis (May) and Charleston (June). In all cases, whites started the violence by attacking political meetings of freed slaves and white Republicans. These were spontaneous explosions of racial hatred aimed at preventing blacks from participating in local politics. 238 pages with a bibliography and an index.

Waskow, Arthur I. *From Race Riot to Sit-In, 1919 and the 1960's: A Study in the Connections Between Conflict and Violence.* Garden City, N.Y.: Doubleday, 1966.
A comparative analysis of the causes of rioting in Chicago and other cities. Discussions of riots in Washington, D.C., Tulsa, and Chicago. Rioting seems to be giving way to other forms of protest, the author concludes a bit prematurely. 380 pages with an index.

Weaver, John D. *The Brownsville Raid.* New York: W. W. Norton, 1970.
A discussion of events concerning the dismissal of 167 African Americans from the U.S. Army. They were dishonorably discharged for refusing to turn in a member of their unit who allegedly had assaulted a white woman. President Theodore Roosevelt refused to review their

case and approved their dismissal. 320 pages with illustrations, references, and an index.

Wiegman, Robyn. *American Anatomies: Theorizing Race and Gender.* Durham, N.C.: Duke University Press, 1995.
A book expressing a feminist view of racial violence. Sees castration as central to lynching, the power given to males is violently deferred from the victims. Chapter 3 concerns "The Anatomy of Lynching." A difficult book. 267 pages with an index.

Williams, Lee E., and Lee E. Williams II. *Anatomy of Four Race Riots: Racial Conflict in Knoxville, Elaine (Arkansas), Tulsa and Chicago, 1919-1921.* Jackson: University and College Press of Mississippi, 1972.
A brief analysis of events leading to four major riots in the aftermath on World War I. White racial hatred inspired the violence and caused most of the deaths. The fear of equality bred intense, destructive hostility. 128 pages with an index.

Zangranado, Robert L. *The NAACP Crusade Against Lynching, 1909-1950.* Philadelphia: Temple University Press, 1980.
A history of one of the few groups pressuring Congress to pass a federal anti-lynching law. Such a law never passed, but the NAACP kept the issue alive by publicizing the immense scale of southern violence. Based on interviews and records. 210 pages with an index.

Chapter 8

RACE AND SEGREGATION, 1877-1920

Anderson, Eric. *Race and Politics in North Carolina, 1872-1901.* Baton Rouge: Louisiana State University Press, 1981.
A history of North Carolina's Second Congressional District, unique because eight of its ten counties had black majorities. From 1874 to 1898, the state sent a black Republican to Congress. By the end of this period, only four blacks remained in the entire House of Representatives. The district was created by the legislature to isolate as many blacks in a single district as possible. The strategy worked as Democrats won the rest of the state's districts. A single black voice in Congress had little influence on legislation. Disfranchisement through literacy tests cost African Americans even this seat after 1900. 372 pages with a statistical appendix, a bibliography, and an index.

Athearn, Robert G. *In Search of Canaan: Black Migration to Kansas, 1879-80.* Lawrence: Regents Press of Kansas, 1978.
Blacks migrated to Kansas in relatively large numbers in 1879 because of the terrible violence they were suffering in the South. As their numbers increased, white Kansans became frightened and confused and began calling for restrictions. Many towns and cities responded by passing segregation laws. 338 pages with maps and an index.

Bailey, Fred Arthur. *Class and Tennessee's Confederate Generation.* Chapel Hill: University of North Carolina Press, 1987.
A study of attitudes of Confederate Army veterans based on a survey done in the 1890's. An analysis of the evidence found in 1,250 questionnaires on economics, education, health, and family structure finds a strong sense of social class identification among these veterans. Contains some information on racial attitudes; not surprisingly, white supremacy dominated.

Bailey, Hugh C. *Liberalism in the New South: Southern Social Reformers and the Progressive Movement.* Coral Gables, Fla.: University of Miami Press, 1969.
Describes careers of George Washington Cable, Booker T. Washington, W. E. B. Du Bois, and Walter Hines Page. Discusses influence of race

and racism in their thought and in the South and how it impeded reform efforts. 290 pages with notes, illustrations, and index.

Beatty, Bess. *A Revolution Gone Backward: The Black Response to National Politics, 1876-1896.* New York: Greenwood Press, 1987.
Politics and race relations from Rutherford B. Hayes to William McKinley. Describes the erosion of black rights as seen by African American journalists and writers. Concludes that the fight for equality was lost by 1896, as even the Republicans turned against equal justice for all and voting rights. 235 pages with notes, a bibliography, and an index.

Bethel, Elizabeth Rauh. *Promiseland: A Century of Life in a Negro Community.* Philadelphia: Temple University Press, 1981.
History of a black community outside of Greenwood, South Carolina, started by fifty families in 1870. Describes with great compassion the strategies devised by African Americans to get along with an unequal place in society. 329 pages with notes, tables, and an index.

Burton, Orville V. *In My Father's House Are Many Mansions: Family and Community in Edgefield, South Carolina.* Chapel Hill: University of North Carolina Press, 1985.
Covers events and changes in family life among African Americans and whites from slavery to the end of 1880's. Race relations under slavery encouraged development of strong African American families, since these were a good means of social control for slave owners. Emancipation led to major changes as freedom threatened white supremacy. Whites turned to violence to maintain control. Blacks were driven out of towns and into the countryside where they would work as low-paid agricultural laborers. These jobs led to extreme poverty and the breakup of families. Women were forced to work as cooks, servants, and washerwomen, fostering rapid disintegration of families. 480 pages with tables, maps, illustrations, notes, a bibliography, and an index.

Callcott, Margaret Law. *The Negro in Maryland Politics, 1870-1912.* Baltimore: The Johns Hopkins University Press, 1969.
A study of how African Americans were excluded from politics. Segregation and denial of rights grew out of the Democratic Party's racist campaign strategy which was successful by 1900. The strategy was successful partly because the Republican Party abandoned the fight for equality. 199 pages with tables and an index.

Cartwright, Joseph H. *The Triumph of Jim Crow: Tennessee Race Relations in the 1880's*. Knoxville: University of Tennessee Press, 1976.
African Americans had gained a high degree of political power by the
early 1880's. By 1890, however, they found themselves segregated,
silenced, and powerless. White attitudes had shifted from paternalism
to hostility and interracial contact practically ended. White Democrats
led the attack in their pursuit of political and economic absolutism. 286
pages with maps and an index.

Casdorph, Paul D. *Republicans, Negroes, and Progressives in the South,
1912-1916*. University: University of Alabama Press, 1981.
A study of Republican Party organization in the eleven states of the
Old Confederacy. A split developed between "lily-whites" and supporters of a black-white coalition. Any move to build an opposition
party seemed doomed, however, as Democrats controlled all the patronage jobs. The result was that no party stood for racial equality and
harmony. 262 pages with notes, a bibliography, and an index.

Cassity, Michael J., ed. *Chains of Fear: American Race Relations Since
Reconstruction*. Westport, Conn.: Greenwood Press, 1984.

_____, ed. *Legacy of Fear: American Race Relations to 1900*. Westport,
Conn.: Greenwood Press, 1985.
Two collections of essays and historical documents containing African
American and white views of racial problems. The essays attempt to
answer question of why white Americans seemed to fear that greater
freedom for African Americans meant a decline in freedom for them.
As long as whites retain this great fear, both peoples will remain unfree.
253 and 274 pages.

Cell, John W. *The Highest Stage of White Supremacy: The Origins of
Segregation in South Africa and the American South*. Cambridge,
England: Cambridge University Press, 1982.
Describes the similarities between segregation in the American South
and apartheid in the Union of South Africa after 1910. Segregation
existed long before it became legal in the southern states just as in South
Africa. Hate preceded law. 288 pages with an index.

Clayton, Bruce. *The Savage Ideal: Intolerance and Intellectual Leadership in the South, 1890-1914*. Baltimore: The Johns Hopkins University Press, 1972.
Examines the ideas of a dozen southerners, intellectuals, writers,
journalists, and clergymen. All were afflicted with racist ideas and

showed a great ignorance of African American life. Concludes, however, that racism was a national characteristic and that white southerners were racist because they were Americans. 231 pages with notes, a bibliographical essay, and an index.

Cohen, William. *At Freedom's Edge: Black Mobility and the Southern White Quest for Racial Control, 1861-1915.* Baton Rouge: Louisiana State University Press, 1991.
A study of the Great Migration from the South to the North and its causes. Blacks moved when they learned of jobs in the North. Whites split on the issue of mobility, some needed black labor and wanted laws limiting movement out of a state. Others wanted to get rid of blacks anyway possible and did not interfere with migration. 340 pages with tables, notes, a bibliography, and an index.

Crockett, Norman L. *The Black Towns.* Lawrence: Regents Press of Kansas, 1979.
A study of voluntary segregation within the confines of all-black communities. Particular attention is paid to five such towns, all of which failed: Nicodemus, Kansas (1879); Mound Bayou, Mississippi (1887); and Langston (1891), Clearview (1903), and Boley (1904) in Oklahoma. All were founded on principles of self-help and moral uplift. The failed because of discrimination and lack of capital to improve roads, schools, and housing. 244 pages with illustrations and an index.

Crow, Jeffrey J., and Flora J. Hatley, eds. *Black Americans in North Carolina and the South.* Chapel Hill: University of North Carolina Press, 1984.
A collection of six essays from a 1981 symposium on black history. The best essay is by Howard Rabinowitz, an urban historian and student of race relations, "A Comparative Perspective on Race Relations in Southern and Northern Cities, 1860-1900, with Special Emphasis on Raleigh" (pages 137-159). Rabinowitz concludes that disfranchisement and discrimination (Jim Crow laws) forced many African Americans to the North in search of a better way of life. 200 pages with tables, illustrations, and an index.

Daniel, Pete. *Breaking the Land: The Transformation of Cotton, Tobacco, and Rice Cultures Since 1880.* Urbana: University of Illinois Press, 1985.
Concentrates on policies of the New Deal in the 1930's and how the Roosevelt Administration decided not to deal with problems of race,

farm ownership, and sharecropping. Blacks applied for relief but had a much more difficult time getting it from local officials than did whites. Whites received $19.51 on average for a family of four while African Americans got $15.17. Blacks, it was argued, knew how to survive on less. There was a widespread belief that relief hurt blacks more than it helped since it would give them a desire to have things they did not need, such as too much food presumably. 352 pages with photographs, notes, and an index.

_____. *The Shadow of Slavery: Peonage in the South, 1901-1969.* New York: Oxford University Press, 1973.
Owing money in the South led to a new kind of slavery for African Americans. Debtors could be imprisoned or put to work for no wages (peonage) until their debts were paid. This practice became a major source of labor in many southern states and proved very difficult to eliminate. 209 pages with illustrations.

_____. *Standing at the Crossroads: Southern Life Since 1900.* New York: Hill & Wang, 1986.
A brief, useful survey of life, politics, and culture. At the turn of the century, it appeared that violence would destroy the South. The potential for racial violence has disappeared and legal segregation had been defeated. Public accommodations have been integrated but most whites and blacks still attend separate churches, recreational facilities, and schools. Vestiges of racism linger in every community, but most white southerners seemed to think they had adjusted well to the changes that went on around them. 259 pages with a bibliographical essay.

DeNevi, Donald P., and Doris A. Holmes, eds. *Racism at the Turn of the Century: Documentary Perspectives, 1870-1910.* San Rafael, Calif.: Leswing Press, 1973.
A collection of essays from original sources, including a number of white supremacist magazines. Includes photographs and brief introductions to each piece by the editors. 403 pages.

Dittmer, John. *Black Georgia in the Progressive Era: 1900-1920.* Urbana: University of Illinois Press, 1977.
Democrats used the race issue to defeat efforts by the Populist Party to unify the poor. White farmers responded to racial appeals rather than to the economic message of the Populists. In "progressive" Georgia, segregation was not merely a line; it became a massive wall. 239 pages with a bibliographical note and an index.

Eagles, Charles W., ed. *The Mind of the South: Fifty Years Later.* Jackson: University of Mississippi Press, 1992.
Eleven essays and commentaries by historians and journalists attending a 1991 celebration of the fiftieth anniversary of the appearance of W. J. Cash's *The Mind of the South.* Bruce Clayton provides a brief biography of the author of one of the most important discussions of white southern attitudes ever presented. Other essays evaluate the importance of the book to history and an understanding of poor white culture. 204 pages with notes and an index.

Edmunds, Helen G. *The Negro and Fusion Politics in North Carolina, 1894-1901.* Chapel Hill: University of North Carolina Press, 1951.
An early assessment that concludes that the white Democratic Party sabotaged a fusion between Populists and Republicans by playing on the race issue. Democrats raised fears of "Negro domination" after fusion candidates won victories in several state contests in 1894 and 1896. White Democrats seized complete control of the state in 1898 by unifying white voters of all economic strata. 260 pages with and index.

Escott, Paul D. *Many Excellent People: Power and Privilege in North Carolina, 1850-1900.* Chapel Hill: University of North Carolina Press, 1985.
Describes attitudes of the white economic and social elite. Finds that Democratic appeals to racial unity drove African Americans and Republicans from power by 1898. Racism became uglier and more violent with each election. Poor whites gained little from the victory of their party. The wealthy elite used political power to advance its own agenda, keeping taxes low and public services to a minimum. This led to a deep distrust of government on the part of lower income white people; it never seemed to do anything for them. 334 pages with illustrations and an index.

Fishwick, Marshall, ed. *Remus, Rastus, Revolution.* Bowling Green, Ohio: Bowling Green University Press, 1970.
A collection of fourteen essays from a conference on images of African Americans in late nineteenth century popular culture. Joseph Boskin, a leading expert of folklore, contributed "The Life and Death of Sambo" (pages 45-57), and Thomas Cripps has a key essay on images in early motion pictures. 165 pages with notes.

Flynn, Charles L., Jr. *White Land, Black Labor: Caste and Class in Late Nineteenth Century Georgia.* Baton Rouge: Louisiana State University Press, 1983.

Landowners dominated Georgia politics and sought wealth through exploitation of white and black sharecroppers. African Americans lived in impoverished independence, while landless whites shared the social privileges of their race, but still lived in great poverty. The author sees poetic retribution in the great poverty afflicting most white Georgians, their racism brought a plague of misery to them and they had earned it. 196 pages with notes, a bibliography, and an index.

Flynt, Wayne. *Poor But Proud: Alabama's Poor Whites.* Tuscaloosa: University of Alabama Press, 1989.

The best book on its subject. Describes the origins of white poverty and describes the lives of tenants, textile workers, miners, and iron workers. Only ideas of racial superiority proved powerful enough to bind whites of different economic classes together. An analysis of how these whites arrived at their low status, and how they coped with extreme economic privation yet retained some dignity. Without racism they would perhaps be more likely to recognize their true status at the bottom of white society. 469 pages with illustrations, notes, a bibliography, and an index.

Fowler, Arlen L. *The Black Infantry in the West, 1869-1891.* Westport Conn.: Greenwood Press, 1971.

A unique discussion of race relations in the U.S. Army during a period of many Indian wars. African American soldiers fought well, followed orders from white officers, and faced discrimination everywhere. Shows that racism was not restricted to the states of the Old Confederacy. 167 pages with an index.

Gaither, Gerald H. *Blacks and the Populist Revolt: Ballots and Bigotry in the "Old South."* University: University of Alabama Press, 1977.

White racism prevented unity between white and black farmers. Race was always more important to whites than was social class or economics. Whites would much rather be poor than share political or social equality with blacks. Alabama Populists hardly supported a radical policy of equality. Instead they approved of Booker T. Washington's philosophy of education and acceptance, for a while, of racial separation. Most whites disliked even that modest program, however, because it implied a future commitment to equality. 251 pages with notes and an index.

Gatewood, Willard B. *Aristocrats of Color: The Black Elite, 1880-1920.*
Bloomington: Indiana University Press, 1990.
Considers class differences within the African American community
in the South. Focuses on the "old families" who viewed themselves as
superior to lower-class blacks in sophistication and achievement. Explores the values, self-image, and culture of the "colored aristocracy."
Includes a portrait of the family of Blanche K. Bruce, an aristocrat of
color, elected for a brief time (1868-1874) to the United States Senate
from Mississippi. 405 pages with photographs, notes, and an index.

_____. *Black Americans and the White Man's Burden, 1898-1903.*
Urbana: University of Illinois Press, 1975.
A discussion of the relation between imperialism and racism and how
African American soldiers and civilians viewed American expansion
into Hawaii, Puerto Rico, and the Philippines. Black Americans were
convinced that all whites were racists including the opponents of
imperial expansion. They saw a great contradiction in efforts by whites
to take up the white man's burden abroad while refusing to help the
less fortunate at home. 352 pages with notes, a bibliography, and an
index.

Gordon, Fon Louise. *Caste and Class: The Black Experience in Arkansas,
1880-1920.* Athens: University of Georgia Press, 1995.
Similar to studies on Georgia and North Carolina, Gordon's work on
Arkansas finds that segregation quickly replaced slavery as the en-
forcer of white supremacy. Still, the African American community had
a class structure of its own that mirrored the social structure of white
America: a very small upper class, an expanding urban middle class,
and a very large rural and urban lower class. Status in African American
society came from family background, lighter skin color, and education. The black middle class stressed self-help and economic independence. Black sharecroppers pushed for economic reform and called
for protest meetings and rallies. The middle class resented these
demands by "the ignorant masses" and felt they were hurting the
advancement of the race. Middle-class blacks preferred separate assimilation within the color line over protesting unequal treatment. A
useful discussion of a frequently ignored topic. 185 pages with notes
and an index.

Graves, John William. *Town and Country: Race Relations in an Urban-
Rural Context: Arkansas, 1865-1905.* Fayetteville: University of Arkansas Press, 1990.

Finds that segregation first appeared in cities on streetcars, in hotels, saloons, parks, and schools. The rural areas did not need legal segregation since fear was enough to keep African Americans in their place. Legal segregation was used to promote and protect white dominance in urban areas. 332 pages with notes, tables, a map, a bibliography, and an index.

Greenwood, Janette Thomas. *Bittersweet Legacy: The Black and White "Better Classes" in Charlotte, 1850-1910.* Chapel Hill: University of North Carolina Press, 1994.
Finds an alliance among educated professionals in Charlotte that suggested an alternative vision of race relations to that provided by the supremacists. Men and women of both races joined across race lines in the 1880's, for instance, to fight for prohibition. This reform alliance collapsed by the 1890's as Jim Crow forced the "better classes" to withdraw, for safety's sake, behind the race line. 318 pages with notes, a map, and an index.

Haller, John S. *Outcasts from Evolution: Scientific Attitudes on Racial Inferiority, 1859-1900.* Urbana: University of Illinois Press, 1976.
Considers how most prominent American physical and social scientists helped to justify the idea of racial inferiority for Africans and Asians. Inferiority of certain races became a scientific "truth." These notions helped justify Jim Crow laws and rigid segregation of Caucasians and "colored" races. 228 pages with illustrations and an index.

Halter, Marilyn. *Between Race and Ethnicity: Cape Verdean American Immigrants, 1860-1965.* Urbana: University of Illinois Press, 1993.
A study of a group never clearly belonging to any racial or ethnic classification. Of mixed African and Portuguese heritage, the Cape Verdeans were the only African peoples to come to the United States voluntarily. They worked in the textile mills and cranberry bogs of Massachusetts. They faced prejudice and discrimination wherever they settled. 213 pages with a bibliography and an index.

Haws, Robert. *The Age of Segregation: Race Relations in the South, 1890-1945.* Jackson: University of Mississippi Press, 1978.
Six essays from a symposium addressing race relations. Derrick Bell considers the legal defenses of inequality in "The Racial Imperative in American Law" (pages 3-28), and Mary Frances Berry treats the subject of violence as a tool of white supremacists in "Repression of Blacks in the South, 1890-1945: Enforcing the System of Segregation" (pages 29-44). Economist Robert Higgs provides evidence showing

how discrimination denied blacks a legitimate return on their labor. A useful set of essays that contains much information. 156 pages with notes.

Hermann, Janet Sharp. *The Pursuit of a Dream.* New York: Oxford University Press, 1981.
The story of a "community of cooperation" that existed at Davis Bend, an all-black plantation in postwar Mississippi. Inspired by Robert Owen's colony at New Harmony, Indiana, former slaves Isaiah and Benjamin Montgomery founded a self-help colony for freedmen in 1888. The two entrepreneurs ad been educated by their owner, Joseph Davis, who saw slavery as a humane enterprise bringing savages to enlightenment. He taught able slaves to read and write. Using their skills as businessmen and farmers, the Montgomerys built their holdings into the third largest plantation in the state by 1895. For more than twenty-five years, until the two brothers died, Davis Bend became a refuge for black success. 290 pages with an index.

Higgs, Robert. *Competition and Coercion: Blacks in the American Economy, 1865-1914.* Cambridge, England: Cambridge University Press, 1977.
An end to slavery did bring some gains for African Americans as some doors were opened to free laborers that were always closed to slaves, such as schooling and the freedom to migrate. Per capita income for African Americans doubled between 1870 and 1900, largely because of skills acquired as farmers, businessmen, and professionals. A useful, positive view of expanding opportunities.

Hirshon, Stanley P. *Farewell to the Bloody Shirt: Northern Republicans and the Southern Negro, 1877-1893.* Bloomington: Indiana University Press, 1962.
Finds Republicans more interested in political concerns than in civil rights for freedmen. Wanted to build the party base on African American votes in the South and maintain the white vote in the North. After the party became a permanent majority in the nation in 1892, it no longer needed African American votes. It dropped all interest in the South because southern whites were firmly entrenched in the Democratic Party. 334 pages with a index.

Inscoe, John C., ed. *Georgia in Black and White: Explorations in Race Relations of a Southern State, 1865-1950.* Athens: University of Georgia Press, 1992.

Eleven essays plus an introduction by the editor. Includes essays on African American women, church leaders, politicians, and educators. Two essays of special interest are Mary Gambrell Rolinson's "The Universal Improvement Association in Georgia" (pages 202-224), which explores Marcus Garvey's "Back to Africa" movement, and Wallace H. Warren's "The Best People in Town Won't Talk," which describes the cover-up of a 1946 lynching in a small Georgia town. 300 pages with notes and an index.

Jaynes, Gerald David. *Branches Without Roots: Genesis of the Black Working Class in the American South, 1862-1882.* New York: Oxford University Press, 1986.
White workers wanted African Americans to stay as agricultural and unskilled laborers. Even in occupations with large numbers of African Americans they received much lower pay. White businesses also relied heavily on convict labor in mines and other unfavorable places. Conditions for these miners were "wretched and appalling." 351 pages with a statistical appendix and an index.

Jones, Jacqueline. *The Dispossessed: America's Underclass from the Civil War to the Present.* New York: Basic Books, 1992.
A general history of people of low material condition, how they got there, and how they have remained poor. African Americans have shown as much, if not more, commitment to education, family, hard work, and morality than any group in the United States. It has not helped most of them because racial attitudes in postindustrial America are little different from those that existed in colonial Virginia. 399 pages with photographs, notes, and an index.

_____. *Labor of Love, Labor of Sorrow: Black Women, Work, and the Family from Slavery to the Present.* New York: Basic Books, 1985.
A general history of black mothers, grandmothers, and others. Explores how they worked, suffered, endured, and held their families together under extremely trying circumstances.

Kenzer, Robert C. *Kinship and Neighborhood in a Southern Community: Orange County, North Carolina, 1849-1881.* Knoxville: University of Tennessee Press, 1987.
A statistical study of one community based on manuscript census returns from the period under discussion. The central theme of life and politics in Orange County, before and after the Civil War, was a desire to give up almost any tradition, custom, or value in order to preserve

white supremacy—the only value that really mattered to them. 251 pages with tables and an index.

Kousser, J. Morgan. *The Shaping of Southern Politics: Suffrage Restriction and the Establishment of the One-Party South, 1880-1910.* New Haven, Conn.: Yale University Press, 1974.
A state-by-state analysis, using many tables of statistical evidence, demonstrating how literacy tests and other methods were used to create a solid white Democratic Party in the South. 267 pages with an index.

Lamon, Lester C. *Black Tennesseans, 1900-1930.* Knoxville: University of Tennessee Press, 1977.
Describes social conditions, racial segregation, and the effects of violence on the African American population. Two separate and unequal communities developed long before the 1960's. 320 pages with an index.

Larson, Edward J. *Sex, Race, and Science: Eugenics in the Deep South.* Baltimore: The Johns Hopkins University Press, 1995.
Explains how the quest for "strong bloodlines" led to scientific experiments and arguments that deeply influenced public policies in education, health care, and social welfare. Scientists "proved" that African Americans were inferior to whites and women were inferior to men.

Lewinson, Paul. *Race, Class, and Party: A History of Negro Suffrage and White Politics in the South.* New York: Grosset & Dunlap, 1965.
A reprint of a 1932 work by a political scientist who surveyed 8,806 "colored citizens." They described the methods and obstacles used by local and state officials to keep blacks from registering to vote. Maintaining white supremacy was always the single most important factor in any white official's conduct. 302 pages with an index.

Lofgren, Charles A. *The Plessy Case: A Legal-Historical Interpretation,* New York: Oxford University Press, 1987.
Argues that in 1896, when the United States Supreme Court rendered its verdict in this most important case involving legal segregation, it simply followed lower court precedents. Since the early 1880's state and federal courts held that legislation permitting racially separate schools and public accommodations was legal as long as they provided relatively equal services or facilities.

Logan, Frenise A. *The Negro in North Carolina, 1876-1894.* Chapel Hill: University of North Carolina Press, 1964.

Finds that African Americans continued to vote in the state into the late 1880's because of protection from the state Supreme Court. Rural African Americans experienced great economic hardships throughout the period. Even in cities, the death rate for African Americans was twice that of whites in the same age categories. Racial prejudice and the need for cheap labor to drain swamps and build railroads led to exploitation and rapid growth of African American prison population. Schools were segregated and white districts received far more state funding than African American districts. 244 pages with an index.

McDonogh, Gary W. *The Florida Negro: A Federal Writers' Project Legacy.* Jackson: University Press of Mississippi, 1993.
A manuscript found by accident that was unpublished for fifty years. A view of race relations from the African American perspective as well as much information on the culture of Florida blacks from the Civil War to the Great Depression. Based on interviews done by workers from the Federal Writers' Project under the direction of Zora Neale Hurston, the famous novelist and folklorist. 177 pages with and index.

McKiven, Henry M., Jr. *Iron and Steel: Class, Race, and Community in Birmingham, Alabama, 1875-1920.* Chapel Hill: University of North Carolina Press, 1995. Describes the oppressive system of racial subordination that arose as African Americans moved into the city to work in its mills. They came seeking freedom from the harsh and extreme violence they found in the countryside. In the city, they found low wages and racial discrimination, but they also found a bit of freedom in their own communities. 290 pages with illustrations, tables, maps, and an index.

McMillen, Neil R. *Dark Journey: Black Mississippians in the Age of Jim Crow.* Urbana: University of Illinois Press, 1989.
The influence of white supremacy on the lives of African Americans from 1865 to 1940. Describes the lynching, reign of terror, and other means used to keep Africans in their place at the very bottom of the economic and social ladder. Includes chapters on "Criminal Justice and Violence" and the beginnings of a protest movement. A well-written survey with a photo essay "Jim Crow's Likeness." 438 pages with notes, tables, maps, and an index.

Mandle, Jay R. *Not Slave, Not Free: The African American Economic Experience Since the Civil War.* Durham, N.C.: Duke University Press, 1992.

A historical explanation of why African American incomes in 1989 averaged only 58.7 percent of white. The fact that most African Americans came from the rural South, the most impoverished region in the United States, was fundamental in accounting for their low incomes. Racial discrimination meant that incomes were even lower than they should have been. Discriminatory hiring in the North kept African Americans contained in the South. Education and job training were quite limited in all areas of the country. 137 pages with tables, notes, and an index.

_____. *The Roots of Black Poverty: The Southern Plantation Economy After the Civil War.* Durham, N.C.: Duke University Press, 1978.
Slavery had been used to keep African Americans dependent on whites. After the war, sharecropping, lynching, and denial of job training or education served the same purpose.

Meier, August. *Negro Thought in America, 1880-1915: Racial Ideologies in the Age of Booker T. Washington.* Ann Arbor: University of Michigan Press, 1964.
A survey of the social thought of leading African American intellectuals during the era of segregation. Describes the debate between Booker T. Washington and W. E. B. Du Bois and the origins of "the New Negro." Also discusses the development of the African American middle class and how it responded to racial separation in the South. 336 pages with an index.

Mencke, John G. *Mulattoes and Race Mixture: American Attitudes and Images, 1865-1918.* Ann Arbor: UMI Research Press, 1979.
Why does the racial system in the United States recognize only two skin colors, white and black? Mixed-bloods are always considered black by white society. In reality, the mulatto is in an unsettled position in both communities. Stratification in the African American social structure places lighter skinned people in the middle or upper class. Culturally they lean toward whites, but racially they are pushed back into black society. This leads to great frustration and mental conflict. Whites treat mixed-bloods as they have always treated Africans, as a distinctly inferior race. One of the better studies of this topic. 267 pages with tables and an index.

Newby, I. A. *Black Carolinians: A History of Blacks in South Carolina from 1895 to 1968.* Columbia: University of South Carolina Press, 1973.

A social and intellectual portrait of African Americans that describes the influence of discrimination, repression, poverty, and racial violence on their lives. 388 pages with an index.

_____, ed. *The Development of Segregationist Thought.* Homewood, Ill.: The Dorsey Press, 1968.
An anthology of readings from segregationist and white supremacist authors. The views of scientists, historians, religious leaders, and politicians on the nature of African "inferiority." The editor includes an epilogue in which he rebuts the claims of the racists. 177 pages.

_____. *Jim Crow's Defense: Anti-Negro Thought in America, 1900-1930.* Baton Rouge: Louisiana State University Press, 1965.
According to Newby, most racists were not hypocrites. They believed everything they wrote and said, no matter how vicious or misguided. They were not crackpots, bigots, or uneducated simpletons, but the cream of southern society. They acted on the assumption that what they said about African Americans was absolutely true. 230 pages with an index.

_____. *Plain Folk in the New South: Social Change and Cultural Persistence, 1880-1915.* Baton Rouge: Louisiana State University Press, 1989.
An analysis of poverty and prejudice based on a reading of hundreds of pages of interviews of white cotton mill workers by the Federal Writer's Project. Exclusion of African Americans from mill work resulted from traditional values of white supremacy. It was sustained by intimidation, coercion, and violence. Whites in mills had little more than racial pride to sustain them. 588 pages with an index.

Nieman, Donald G., ed. *The Constitution, Law, and American Life: Critical Aspects of the Nineteenth Century Experience.* Athens: University of Georgia Press, 1992.
Papers from a 1989 symposium at New York University, including Nieman's "The Language of Liberation: African Americans and Equalitarian Constitutionalism, 1830-1950" (pages 67-90). Antebellum African Americans challenged slavery by referring to ideas of citizenship, due process, and equality. These ideas were also a potent weapon in the struggle for civil rights. 197 pages with an index.

_____. *Plain Folk in the New South: Social Change and Cultural Persistence, 1880-1915.* Baton Rouge: Louisiana State University Press, 1989.

An analysis of poverty and prejudice based on a reading of hundreds of pages of interviews of white cotton mill workers by the Federal Writers' Project. Exclusion of African Americans from mill work resulted from traditional values of white supremacy. It was sustained by intimidation, coercion, and violence. Whites in mills had little more than racial pride to sustain them. 588 pages with an index.

Nolen, Claude H. *The Negro's Image in the South: The Anatomy of White Supremacy.* Lexington: University of Kentucky Press, 1968.
Covers the period from 1865 to 1914. A political and psychological portrait of white supremacists. Their biblical defense of slavery transferred easily to a view of freedmen. African Americans were lazy and criminal, that is why slavery had been necessary. Scientists, both social and biological, showed that Africans were creatures of their feelings. They were dull witted and weak of will. Freedom only gave them a opportunity to roam about wild whereas as slaves they had at least been controlled. 232 pages with an index.

Olsen, Otto H., ed. *The Thin Disguise: Turning Point in Negro History, Plessy v. Ferguson, A Documentary Presentation.* New York: Humanities Press, 1967.
With an introduction by the editor placing the famous case in historical perspective. Includes the full background of the case, with legal briefs, newspaper accounts and editorials, plus lower court decisions. 132 pages with notes.

Painter, Nell Irwin. *Exodusters: Black Migration to Kansas After Reconstruction.* New York: Alfred A. Knopf, 1977.
The story of twenty thousand freedmen who fled from the terrors of Mississippi and other southern states to the plains of Kansas. Even here, however, they were segregated in schools and found discriminatory hiring practices. Most remained very poor, but by 1900, they were better off than the sharecroppers left behind in the South. 288 pages with illustrations and an index.

Powers, Bernard E., Jr. *Black Charlestonians: A Social History, 1822-1865.* Fayetteville: University of Arkansas Press, 1994.
A survey of the social and economic evolution of the African American population, from slavery to freedom. Discusses the establishment of schools, churches, unions, sports clubs, and businesses. Includes an analysis of the sharp social and class divisions within the community and how African Americans of all classes responded to war and freedom. 377 pages with tables, notes, a bibliography, and an index.

Rabinowitz, Howard N. *The First New South, 1865-1920*. Arlington
Heights, Ill.: Harlan Davidson, 1992.
A brief survey of the South after the Civil War and the development of
Jim Crow. 128 pages with an index.

_____. *Race, Ethnicity, and Urbanization: Selected Essays*. Columbia:
University of Missouri Press, 1994.
A collection of the author's essays from various historical journals.
Argues that segregation replaced the racial exclusion found under
slavery and if it had truly been equal it would have been a major
advance. Contains an especially interesting article on "Historians and
Segregation," and another on "The Weight of the Past vs. The Promise
of the Future: Southern Race Relations" (pages 318-340). Separate but
equal quickly led to separate but unequal facilities and rights. 359 pages
with an index.

_____. *Race Relations in the Urban South, 1865-1890*. New York:
Oxford University Press, 1978.
Why did segregation emerge? One of the most balanced and humane
treatments of the subject. Blacks and whites accepted or requested
segregated facilities. For African Americans, even an inferior second-
class citizenship was an advance over slavery. Any other choice would
have further alienated an already hostile white population. Segregation
for whites promoted their self-worth and esteem and prevented social
equality and intermarriage. Racial separation kept poor whites happy
and allowed the wealthy elite to maintain power and control. 441 pages
with maps, tables, notes, an excellent bibliographic essay, and an index.

Rachleff, Peter J. *Black Labor in the South: Richmond, Virginia, 1865-
1890*. Philadelphia: Temple University Press, 1984.
Describes efforts by early unions, including the Knights of Labor, to
organize interracial coalitions of workers. All efforts to eliminate the
color line failed. The failure of Populists, Socialists, and unions to cross
racial barriers testified to the enormous significance of race in social
and economic relations. Little else mattered but skin color, and separated peoples soon became hostile peoples. 249 pages with notes and
an index.

Rice, Lawrence D. *The Negro in Texas: 1874-1900*. Baton Rouge: Louisiana State University Press, 1971.
Finds that the race issue was seldom absent from post-Civil War politics
in Texas. Emancipation brought freedom, poverty, and legal separation
through Jim Crow laws. 309 pages with a bibliography and an index.

Rosengarten, Theodore, comp. *All God's Dangers: The Life of Nate Shaw.* New York: Avon, 1974.
A black sharecropper (Ned Cobb) shares his life, including his effort to pursue the American Dream on individualism and property owner-ship in rural Alabama in the first half of the twentieth century. A vivid and memorable oral history.

Shankman, Arnold. *Ambivalent Friends: Afro-Americans View the Immi-grant.* Westport, Conn.: Greenwood Press, 1982.
Offers African Americans' views of Chinese, Japanese, Mexican, Ital-ian, and Jewish immigration into the southern part of the United States based on a reading of African American newspapers and magazines. African American laundry workers, porters, field hands, and barbers worried mostly about job competition; immigration posed a real threat. Moreover, immigrants seemed to have rights that were always denied to African Americans. Jews were not as mistrusted by southern blacks because they posed less of a menace to the unskilled occupations filled by blacks. 189 pages with notes, tables, and a index.

Shifflett, Crandall A. *Patronage and Poverty in the Tobacco South: Louisa County, Virginia, 1860-1900.* Knoxville: University of Tennessee Press, 1982.
African Americans had limited access to jobs. They were poor because they were black. Black poverty was assumed to be merely the natural order of things by whites. Anyone who tried to violate this principle of universal law was met with violence and intimidation and frequently death. 159 pages with a statistical appendix, notes, and an index.

Smith, John David. *The Eugenic Assault on America: Scenes in Red, White, and Black.* Fairfax, Va.: George Mason University Press, 1993.
A study of the crusade for sterilization of racial degenerates, especially those of a "criminal nature." In the author's view, eugenics was genocide, and the Nazis learned their racial theories from the move-ment that originated in the United States. The U.S. Supreme Court defended sterilization in 1927, *Buck v. Bell*, arguing that "three genera-tions of imbeciles is enough." 116 pages with an index.

———. *An Old Creed for the New South: Proslavery Ideology and Historiography, 1865-1918.* Westport, Conn.: Greenwood Press, 1985.
Explores the image of black slavery in American thought. Historians of the period extolled the virtues of slavery although none advocated reenslavement. History reinforced the ideas of white supremacy. Early

black writers began to challenge this view but were seldom taken seriously. 314 pages with a bibliography and an index.

_____, ed. *Racial Determinism and the Fear of Miscegenation, Pre-1900: Race and the Negro Problem*. Vol. 1. New York: Garland, 1993.
A collection of essays by various historians with a general introduction by the editor. Essays by George Fredrickson, "Selfishness, Greed, and the Pursuit of Privilege," and Joel Williamson, "A Rage for Order," are especially pertinent. This is the first volume of an eleven-volume anthology of documents related to racist thought from 1863 to 1925. The series includes complete texts of eighty-six racist books, pamphlets, and essays. The volumes are arranged by theme: backwardness, inferiority, the horrors of Reconstruction, fear of interracial marriage, and other themes.

Sochen, June. *The Unbridgeable Gap: Blacks and Their Quest for the American Dream, 1900-1930*. Chicago: Rand McNally, 1972.
Discusses African American writers and intellectuals and how the myth of economic success continued to motivate them despite great political, economic, and social discrimination. 136 pages with an index.

Sosna, Morton. *In Search of the Silent South*. New York: Columbia University Press, 1977.
A consideration of southern whites who recognized the injustice of racial prejudice and discrimination. Newspaper editors and writers such as Walter Hines Page, Virginius Dabney, and Lillian Smith called for a nonracist approach to life, but they also urged a good deal of caution on the way. They apparently felt little urgency in the plight of African Americans. Covers the period from 1890 to 1920, the "grimmest period" in the history of southern race relations. 275 pages with notes and an index.

Tindall, George B. *The Ethnic Southerners*. Baton Rouge: Louisiana State University Press, 1976.
A collection of the historian's essays from 1958 to 1975. The most important is "The Central Theme Revisited" (pages 59-87), an analysis of racism in southern culture. African Americans were depicted as beasts long after the Civil War was over, and slavery was seen as a civilizing process by whites well into the twentieth century. 251 pages with an index.

_____. *South Carolina Negroes: 1877-1900*. Columbia: University of South Carolina Press, 1952.

The creation of a caste system based on race is described. Slavery was replaced as an instrument of maintaining subordination of African Americans by a system of physical segregation maintained by law, terror, and lynching. There was little contact between blacks and whites after 1877. 336 pages with an index.

Toll, William. *The Resurgence of Race: Black Social Theory from Reconstruction to the Pan-African Conferences.* Philadelphia: Temple University Press, 1979.

Covers the period from 1877 to 1920. Primarily involved with the debate between Booker T. Washington and W. E. B. Du Bois over tactics. How should African Americans respond to the devastating attacks upon their character and personality launched by white supremacists? One side counseled temporary acceptance in preparation for equality in the future while the other side advised forceful and immediate action. 270 pages with an index.

Turner, William H., and Edward J. Cabbell. *Blacks in Appalachia.* Lexington: University Press of Kentucky, 1985.

Essays on red-white-black relations by historians, political scientists, and sociologists. Describes the roots of prejudice and economic inequality. "Black Invisibility and Racism in Appalachia" (pages 3-10) is a fine essay that summarizes the contents of the book. 277 pages with tables.

Wacker, R. Fred. *Ethnicity, Pluralism, and Race: Race Relations Theory in America Before Myrdal.* Westport, Conn.: Greenwood Press, 1983.

A survey of sociological ideas in the 1920's with particular attention to the "Chicago School" of Robert E. Park, Everett Hughes, and others. They were assimilationists who believed African Americans were exactly like other immigrant groups in American society. Conflict resulted when a system of race relations, such as slavery, broke down and there was nothing to replace it. Ultimately a racial caste system emerged that would be quite difficult to change. 114 pages with an index.

Wayne, Michael. *The Reshaping of Plantation Society: The Natchez District, 1860-1880.* Baton Rouge: Louisiana State University Press, 1983.

A study of the richest district in the Cotton South. Methods used by planters and merchants of the New South to control freedmen were the same as were used to control white tenants, high credit, crop liens, mortgages, and the manipulation of prices. The Old Gentry held onto its place by convincing poor whites that race was more important in life than anything else, even prosperity. 226 pages with tables and an index.

Wharton, Vernon L. *The Negro in Mississippi, 1865-1890.* Chapel Hill: University of North Carolina Press, 1947.
One of the first postwar works on African American history. Segregation was always part of the system. Describes how the politics of race dominated the political culture and how violence pushed African Americans into second-class status. 298 pages with an index.

White, Ronald C., Jr. *Liberty and Justice for All: Racial Reform and the Social Gospel (1877-1925).* New York: Harper & Row, 1990.
Finds that many ministers preaching the Social Gospel, that Christians had responsibilities for less fortunate people, participated in movements for racial reform. Black and white clergymen were active in the NAACP and the Urban League. 309 pages with an index.

Williams, Vernon J., Jr. *From a Caste to a Minority: Changing Attitudes of American Sociologists Toward Afro-Americans, 1896-1945.* New York: Greenwood Press, 1989.
How and why did sociology turn from a social science that described caste-like arrangements, and sometimes defended them, to one that advocated assimilation? A study of the movement against Social Darwinism that slowly emerged in the profession. 202 pages with an index.

Wilson, Charles Reagan. *Baptized in Blood: The Religion of the Lost Cause, 1865-1920.* Athens: University of Georgia Press, 1980.
Race was of fundamental importance in keeping the myth of white unity alive. Africans needed moral and social discipline, something slavery provided. This study of Ku Klux Klan and "liberal" ministers describes how "racial heresy," which could be anything close to a call for humane treatment for blacks, was more dangerous to express than any type of theological speculation no matter how ridiculous. 256 pages with notes and an index.

Wright, George C. *Life Behind a Veil: Blacks in Louisville, Kentucky, 1865-1930.* Baton Rouge: Louisiana State University Press, 1985.
The story of "polite racism" as experienced in a city with no lynchings or race riots. Yet, African Americans were considered inferior and in need of moral guidance by the white upper class. Politeness existed a long as African Americans stayed in their place, at the bottom of

society. Segregation was maintained though in a less violent form than in many other southern communities. 302 pages with notes, maps, tables, and an index.

Wynes, Charles E., ed. *The Negro in the South Since 1865: Selected Essays in American Negro History.* University: University of Alabama Press, 1965. Reprint. New York: Harper & Row, 1968.
Eleven essays by leading historians. Includes John Hope Franklin's "Jim Crow Goes to School: The Genesis of Legal Segregation in the South" (pages 135-148). Philip Durham and Everett L. Jones also provide useful information in "Negro Cowboys" (pages 219-230).

_____. *Race Relations in Virginia, 1870-1902.* Totowa, N.J.: Rowman & Littlefield, 1971.
Race relations in the state deteriorated markedly during the period under discussion. African Americans were increasingly used, abused, and finally driven from the polls by whites. 164 pages with an index.

Chapter 9

RACE RELATIONS IN PROSPERITY, DEPRESSION, AND WAR

1920-1960

Bartley, Numan V. *The Rise of Massive Resistance: Race and Politics in the South During the 1950's.* Baton Rouge: Louisiana State University Press, 1969.
A work that contains the full story of the rise of "massive resistance" to the Supreme Court's 1954 *Brown* decision ordering an end to legal segregation. White Citizens Councils rose up throughout the South to fight the court order and resist federal "interference" in local affairs. A rich and detailed history

Bass, Jack. *Unlikely Heroes: The Southern Judges Who Made the Civil Rights Revolution.* Tuscaloosa: University of Alabama Press, 1990.
Originally published in 1981, this work tells the story of federal judges on the Fifth Circuit Court of Appeals in New Orleans. Under the leadership of Judge Frank M. Johnson, Jr., they expanded the meaning of the Fourteenth Amendment to include the concept of equality and concluded that the effects of past discrimination were worthy of special consideration in court cases. Based on taped interviews with the judges involved, the book explains the difficulties faced by judges who were accused by many of being traitors to their white race. 352 pages with an index.

Bass, Jack, and Walter De Vries. *The Transformation of Southern Politics: Social Change and Political Consequence Since 1945.* New York: Basic Books, 1976.
A state-by-state analysis of voting patterns in local and national elections. Race was the major problem and issue dividing voters. The book is superseded by Earl and Merle Black's *Politics and Society in the South* (1987), cited below. Includes graphs, maps, and an index. 527 pages.

Berman, William C. *The Politics of Civil Rights in the Truman Administration.* Columbus: Ohio State University Press, 1970.

A discussion of progress made in race relations under the first president to have a civil rights program. A discussion of the political bravery involved in announcing Executive Order 9981 providing for desegregation of the armed forces. This was President Harry Truman's greatest civil rights achievement. It provided only token gains politically but was a true breakthrough for African Americans and challenged traditional stereotypes. 261 pages with notes and an index.

Berry, Faith, ed. *A Scholar's Conscience: Selected Writings of J. Saunders Redding, 1942-1977.* Lexington: University Press of Kentucky, 1992. Includes the major essays of a leading black historian, novelist, biographer, and critic. 238 pages with an index.

Black, Earl, and Merle Black. *Politics and Society in the South.* Cambridge, Mass.: Harvard University Press, 1987.
A vast survey of elections, issues, and personalities that influenced southern history from 1920 to 1985. A major discussion of changes in race relations from a time of extreme segregation to the fight against desegregation in the post-1960's era. Although surveys found a wide variety of differences among whites in their attitudes toward education, economics, and foreign policy on one thing there was a great feeling of unity, blacks had to be kept in their place. There was no "progressive" white minority pushing for racial equality. On questions such as affirmative action, whites and blacks stood at opposite poles. A wealth of information on every issue of public policy, and every key election, over a sixty-five-year period. 363 pages with maps, charts, graphs, and an index.

Blauner, Bob. *Racial Oppression in America.* New York: Harper & Row, 1972.
A major challenge to traditional sociological views of race relations. African Americans were treated more harshly and exposed to more hatred than any other group in the United States. They deserved special treatment because they had been especially abused. An angry, intense book that avoids the usual sociological jargon.

Bogart, Leo, ed. *Social Research and Desegregation of the United States Army.* Chicago: Markham, 1969.
Contains two original reports first issued in 1951 on the effects of President Harry Truman's order desegregating American armed forces. The first, "The Utilization of Negro Troops in Korea," looks at the first units sent to that war on a integrated basis. The second report reviews "The Utilization of Negro Troops in the Continental United States."

Both reports conclude that integration "worked." Desegregation could work if it was backed by people in command and it is was planned to avoid "tipping" a unit. In that case, "too many" blacks in a unit would cause resentment on the part of whites. 393 pages with tables and an index.

Bunche, Ralph J. *The Political Status of the Negro in the Age of FDR.* Edited by Dewey W. Grantham. Chicago: University of Chicago Press, 1973.
Contains the uncompleted first draft of a work based on more than five hundred field interviews conducted by students and staff from Howard University in the 1930's. The future United Nations delegate led the research team but was unable to complete the project. Many of the findings were later used by Gunnar Myrdal for his investigation of American race relations. It includes interviews with whites and African Americans and reveals much about attitudes on race relations in the South. 682 pages with an index.

Burgess, M. Elaine. *Negro Leadership in a Southern City.* Chapel Hill: University of North Carolina Press, 1960.
An old fashioned sociological study of "Crescent City," an otherwise unidentified city in the Middle South. It had a population of eighty thousand in the 1950's, and was 35 percent African American. Provides an analysis of the traditional black leadership class of ministers and businessmen. White leaders seemed interested in broadening the power structure to include representatives of the whole community. Both black and white leaders feared the "lower class" (race did not matter here) and tried to cooperate to maintain "responsible" control. 231 pages with tables, figures, and an index.

Burk, Robert Frederick. *The Eisenhower Administration and Black Civil Rights.* Knoxville: University of Tennessee Press, 1984.
Reveals that the Republican leadership had genuine concerns about the constitutional legitimacy of civil rights claims, such as school desegregation and voting rights. Eisenhower seemed willing to act only in those areas of law he believed were directly under presidential control—in other words, only in the armed forces. School and voting rights were areas best left to state authorities. 282 pages with an index.

Capeci, Dominic J., Jr. *Race Relations in Wartime Detroit: The Sojourner Truth Housing Controversy of 1942.* Philadelphia: Temple University Press, 1984.

Traces events leading to the great Detroit race riot of 1943. A detailed analysis of the violence and prejudice in the city prior to that catastrophe.

Clayton, Bruce, and John A. Salmond, eds. *The South Is Another Land: Essays on the Twentieth Century South.* New York: Greenwood Press, 1987.
Includes ten essays and an introduction by the editors. Subjects include politics, work, religion, and the "Southern mind." Emphasizes how the South was different from the rest of the United States. The South mandated white supremacy, it was natural, and had to be accepted. Several short biographies of key segregationists are included, such as James F. Byrnes and Senator Clyde R. Hoey, two influential exploiters of the race issue. 216 pages with notes and an index.

Cobb, James C. *The Most Southern Place on Earth: The Mississippi Delta and the Roots of Regional Identity.* New York: Oxford University Press, 1992.
Looks for the causes of African American poverty, the origins of stereotypes, the acceptance of inferior schools, and the resistance to voter registration from plantation days to the 1980's. Finds a white society in the Delta where material success counted whatever the human and social costs. African Americans suffered greatly and made huge sacrifices for the sake of their children but whites hardly paid any attention at all. 391 pages with notes and an index.

_____. *The Selling of the South: The Southern Crusade for Industrial Development, 1936-1980.* Baton Rouge: Louisiana State University Press, 1982.
Progress on race relations had little or no influence on corporate decisions to locate in the South. Interviews with more than three hundred business leaders in southern states found not a single one who favored an end to segregation. They opposed the physical violence of the anti-civil rights forces, but if segregation could have been maintained by peaceful means they would have little trouble with it. 309 pages with an index.

Cruse, Harold. *The Crisis of the Negro Intellectual: A Historical Analysis of the Failure of Black Leadership.* New York: William Morrow, 1967.
One of the most important books on race relations to come out of the 1960's by a black scholar. Sees African American history as a cycle of conflict between integrationist and nationalist forces. Extremely criti-

cal of separatist and Black Power ideas because they lack any sense of reality, history, or intelligence. 594 pages with an index.

Dalfiume, Richard M. *Desegregation of the United States Armed Forces: Fighting on Two Fronts, 1939-1953.* Columbia: University of Missouri Press, 1969.
The best of several works on this topic. A detailed analysis of the African American experience in World War II and Korea. Places Harry Truman's famous Executive Order 9981 in historical and political perspective. 290 pages with an index.

Davidson, Chandler. *Race and Class in Texas Politics.* Princeton, N.J.: Princeton University Press, 1990.
A sociologist reviews Texas politics in the 1980's and finds a state still torn by racial and class conflict dating to the Civil War era. The clash had tragic consequences for a state with one of the largest poverty populations in the nation. The business elite controlling the state made Texas last among all fifty states in per capita spending on all government programs. It was twenty-ninth in education spending, forty-ninth in welfare, and last again in spending for alcohol and drug abuse programs. The only solution would be an end to racial politics, but how could that ever come about when one party saw an electoral advantage in fanning the flames of racial hatred? 344 pages with photographs, notes, and an index.

Fisher, Paul L., and Ralph L. Lowenstein. *Race and the News Media.* New York: Frederick A. Praeger, 1967.
Papers from the annual conference of the Freedom of Information Center at the University of Missouri. Essays on news coverage of riots and "The Racial Crisis and the News Media." On pages 25-36, Martin Hayden considers the bloodiest of all the riots and how newspaper coverage missed most of the important events in "Reporting the Racial Story in Detroit." An interesting collection of views by journalists and critics. 158 pages.

Foner, Jack D. *Blacks and the Military in American History.* New York: Frederick A. Praeger, 1974.
A survey of African Americans in the military from the American Revolution to Vietnam. Covers all the wars and the steps toward desegregation. 374 pages with an index.

Franklin, Raymond S. *Shadows of Race and Class.* Minneapolis: University of Minnesota Press, 1991.

A discussion of social class relations among African Americans from 1950 to 1990. Overcrowding of blacks in the lower class cast a shadow on middle-class members of the race. They have good credentials for middle-class professions but are excluded or discriminated against in business and society on racial grounds. Equality in income and jobs that break through these patterns of discrimination are required for the elimination of racism. 189 pages with an index.

Fraser, Walter J., Jr., and Winfred B. Moore, Jr., eds. *From the Old South to the New: Essays on the Transitional South.* Westport, Conn.: Greenwood Press, 1981.
A collection of essays on a variety of topics including race relations. Especially interesting is James A. Burrow's "Urban Racial Violence in the South During World War II: A Comparative Overview."

Garfinkel, Herbert. *When Negroes March: The March on Washington Movement in the Organizational Politics for the FEPC.* Glencoe, Ill.: The Free Press, 1959.
A discussion of the March on Washington planned for July, 1941, to secure passage of a bill creating the Fair Employment Practices Commission. The March on Washington movement captured a great deal of enthusiasm among middle-class African Americans. This book presents an organizational history of the movement and its leaders. 224 pages with notes and an index.

Garrow, David J., ed. *We Shall Overcome: The Civil Rights Movement in the United States in the 1950's and the 1960's.* 3 vols. Brooklyn, N.Y.: Carlson Publishing, 1989.
A three-volume collection of fifty-two articles and essays on all aspects of the Civil Rights movement, from organization to philosophy, tactics, successes, and losses. Introduced by the editor. Each essay is placed in its historical perspective. 1,175 pages.

Glazer, Nathan, and Daniel P. Moynihan. *Beyond the Melting Pot: The Negroes, Puerto Ricans, Jews, Italians and Irish of New York City.* Cambridge, Mass.: MIT Press, 1963.
An award-winning sociological study that concludes that the "melting-pot" never happened. This discussion of New York City's principal ethnic groups finds that they continued to live in separate communities, perpetuating traditional values, and maintaining traditional religions. Also discusses the levels of achievement of each group and provides a brief overview of ethnic and racial politics in the city. 360 pages with an index.

Goings, Kenneth W. *"The NAACP Comes of Age:" The Defeat of Judge John J. Parker.* Bloomington: Indiana University Press, 1990.

Details how the NAACP launched a campaign in 1930 to defeat a southern white Republican nominated to the Supreme Court by President Herbert Hoover. The lobbying effort became a rallying point for liberals and reinvigorated the civil rights community in the aftermath of the defeat of the Dyer Anti-Lynching Bill. 125 pages with notes, a bibliography, and an index.

Goldfield, David R. *Black, White, and Southern: Race Relations and Southern Culture, 1940 to the Present.* Baton Rouge: Louisiana State University Press, 1990.

A major historical analysis of race relations from the beginning of World War II to the mid-1980's. The races had lived together side by side for centuries but never got to know each other. Discusses the etiquette of race relations that demanded black subservience and white control. Whites expected blacks to be oversexed, stupid, lethargic, and above all happy. African Americans had to be invisible, and "happy," in order to survive. Their powerlessness generated shame, guilt, frustration, and self-hatred, that was sometimes released through violence, usually black-on-black violence. In the white community, racial solidarity was used to cover up terrible economic and social disparities. Prevailing racial attitudes during this period lead Goldfield to conclude that very little had changed since slavery days. 321 pages with an excellent bibliographic essay, illustrations, and an index.

Grantham, Dewey W. *The Life and Death of the Solid South: A Political History.* Lexington: University Press of Kentucky, 1988.

A general history from the end of Reconstruction to the 1980's. Sees the New Deal as a major turning-point since it broke the power of the plantation elite. It failed, however, to deal with racial issues and black-white cleavages continued to dominate politics. The white middle class was the major beneficiary of the new economic and political forces changing the South. Yet race dominated their thinking, too, just as it had the planter elite. The African American minority had benefited little from the change. 257 pages with notes and an index.

Hine, Darlene Clark. *Black Victory: The Rise and Fall of the White Primary in Texas.* Millwood, N.Y.: KTO Press, 1979.

A good, detailed account of the famous Supreme Court case finding the "whites only" Democratic primary system in Texas (and other states) an unconstitutional violation of rights of citizens. One of the first and most significant victories for the NAACP and other groups fighting racism in American politics.

_____. *When the Truth Is Told: Black Women's Culture and Community in Indiana, 1875-1950.* Bloomington: Indiana University Press, 1981. A history of black women in Indiana with special emphasis on women's involvement in churches.

Hirsch, Arnold R. *Making of the Second Ghetto: Race and Housing in Chicago, 1940-1960.* New York: Cambridge University Press, 1983. A history of public housing, real estate development, and the fight over integration in Chicago, especially the Hyde Park community around the University of Chicago. Discusses the origins and aftermath of several violent incidents in the Chicago Housing Authority's campaign to desegregate the city's public housing. Also contains much useful information on city politics, especially the careers of Chicago mayors Martin Kennelly and Richard J. Daley. 281 pages with an index.

Horne, Gerald. *Communist Front? The Civil Rights Congress, 1946-1956.* Rutherford, N.J.: Fairleigh Dickinson University Press, 1988. A lengthy survey of the history of an organization labeled Communist by Senator Joseph McCarthy, J. Edgar Hoover, and other luminaries of the anti-Communist crusade during the Eisenhower years. The author finds many Communists working in and for groups pressing for equality, including the Civil Rights Congress. They did not, however, engage in espionage or in any way threaten national security. Instead, most Communist Party members seemed dedicated to the cause of equal justice in the United States. 454 pages with notes and index.

Katznelson, Ira. *Black Men, White Cities: Race, Politics, and Migration in the United States, 1900-1930 and Britain, 1948-1968.* New York: Oxford University Press, 1973. A study in comparative racial politics. Also looks at how democratic states deal with race relations during periods of turmoil and urban expansion. Concentrates on New York City, Chicago, and Nottingham. 219 pages with an index.

Keppel, Ben. *The Work of Democracy: Ralph Bunche, Kenneth B. Clark, Lorraine Hansberry, and the Cultural Politics of Race.* Cambridge, Mass.: Harvard University Press, 1995. Concentrates on the years 1935 to 1965 and the work and art of diplomat, a social scientist, and a playwright. Who was "in" in the African American community and who was "out" as defined by these

African American leaders. Also describes the burdens and difficulties placed on the personal lives and fortunes of "role models." 314 pages with notes and an index.

Key, V. O., Jr. *Southern Politics in State and Nation.* New York: Alfred A. Knopf, 1949.
The classic study by the great political scientist of southern political leadership, mainly white, in the early postwar period. Interesting interviews with some of the staunchly white supremacist leaders on the state and local level. Race infects the political views of all politicians, voters, and leaders.

King, Richard H. *A Southern Renaissance: The Cultural Awakening of the American South, 1930-1955.* New York: Oxford University Press, 1980.
Although primarily a literary study, King's work does include some useful comments on racial influences in the writings of William Faulkner, Thomas Wolfe, and others.

Kirby, Jack Temple. *Rural Worlds Lost: The American South, 1920-1960.* Baton Rouge: Louisiana State University Press, 1987.
Focuses on social disruption and economic distress caused by the Great Depression and its aftermath, especially the decline of plantation agriculture and the disappearance of many sharecroppers from the land. Includes a discussion of racial attitudes and how they varied across class and regional lines.

Kirby, John B. *Black Americans in the Roosevelt Era: Liberalism and Race.* Knoxville: University of Tennessee Press, 1980.
Describes the ideas and influence of a small group of integrationists, including Harold Ickes, Eleanor Roosevelt, Will Alexander, A. Philip Randolph, and Walter White. The accepted the belief, later promoted by Gunnar Myrdal, that a favorable change in white attitudes or an improvement in African American standards of living would lead to less conflict and prejudice. Racism would diminish as African Americans improved their economic status. Changes along these lines did not produce these results as prejudice remained a major problem in spite of some economic advance. 254 pages with an index.

Kluger, Richard. *Simple Justice: The History of Brown v. Board of Education and Black America's Struggle for Equality.* New York: Alfred A. Knopf, 1976

A massive, detailed, extremely well-written history of race relations in the United States from the 1890's to 1955. Based on dozens of interviews and documentary sources. A history of all the violence, protests, and eventual success of the NAACP Legal Defense and Education Fund's fight against legal segregation. 824 pages with photographs, notes, and an index.

Kneebone, John T. *Southern Liberal Journalists and the Issue of Race, 1920-1944.* Chapel Hill: University of North Carolina Press, 1985.
A study of the work and influence of five journalists who had great influence on the South's changing racial patterns. Gerald W. Johnson, George Fort Milton, Virginius Dabney, Ralph McGill, and Hodding Carter all desired to improve the region's race relations to promote southern chances for economic development and progress. 312 pages with a bibliographical note and an index.

Krueger, Thomas A. *And Promises to Keep: The Southern Conference for Human Welfare, 1938-1948.* Nashville: Vanderbilt University Press, 1967.
A study of an important voluntary organization of white liberals devoted to fighting racial and religious prejudice. The conference supported an anti-lynching law and other civil rights causes but because some of its members were involved with the Communist Party it fell victim to the anti-Red hysteria of the early Cold War. 218 pages with an index.

Ladd, Everett Carll. *Negro Political Leadership in the South.* Ithaca, N.Y.: Cornell University Press, 1966.
A study of African American church and civic leaders in Winston-Salem and Greenville, North Carolina, from 1946 to the early 1960's by a leading student of public opinion and American politics. Tries to answer two questions: What do African American leaders want and how do they propose to get it? An interesting display of pre-Civil Rights era African American thinking on race relations. 348 pages with tables and an index.

Lamis, Alexander P. *The Two-Party South.* New York: Oxford University Press, 1988.
Finds that in the 1970's whites generally accepted integration and Democrats were successful in building a very fragile black-white coalition. Racial divisions began to grow in the 1980's, however, as Republicans played the race card and aligned with some African American politicians to establish black majority districts, a policy that

split the Democrats and created a majority of heavily white-dominated Republican congressional districts. A state-by-state analysis of election returns through 1986. 408 pages with maps, tables, and an index.

Lawson, Steven F. *Black Ballots: Voting Rights in the South, 1944-1969.* New York: Columbia University Press, 1976.
A key study of the impact of the voting rights movement in the South and the final overthrow of Jim Crow registration policies. Illustrates the impact of the Voting Rights Act of 1965, which outlawed the major impediment to equal registration—the literacy test. 348 pages with charts, tables, and an index.

Lee, Frank F. *Negro and White in Connecticut Town.* New York: Bookman Associates, 1961.
A rarity, a sociological study of race relations in a northern industrial town in the early 1950's. The town (unnamed by the author) considered itself liberal on questions of race relations. In reality, however, there was a wide disparity between blacks and whites. African Americans faced subordination and exclusion in every aspect of their lives, whether education, employment, or recreation. Based on personal observations, interviews, and documents. 207 pages with an index.

Lisio, Donald J. *Hoover, Blacks, and Lily-Whites: A Study of Southern Strategies.* Chapel Hill: University of North Carolina Press, 1985.
Herbert Hoover did not share the racism of many Republican leaders in the 1920's. He rejected the policy offered by "lily-whites," who sought to exclude African Americans from party involvement in the South. He supported real political power for blacks and believed that with economic progress racism would eventually die out. His biggest mistake was to underestimate the power of racism in American life. Not even economic progress would bring an end to it. 372 pages with a bibliographical essay and an index.

McCoy, Donald R. *Quest and Response: Minority Rights and the Truman Administration.* Lawrence: University Press of Kansas, 1973.
A study of the great advances made toward equal rights during the Truman years, 1945-1952. Finds that the racial violence of 1946 regenerated the movement toward racial progress in the White House. Truman listened to minority group leaders as no president had done before. The president's agenda helped bring an end to legal segregation in the military and in education and employment. 427 pages with an index.

McMillen, Neil R. *The Citizens Council: Organized Resistance to the Second Reconstruction.* Urbana: University of Illinois Press, 1971.
Describes the rise and fall of the major group organized to fight school desegregation in the 1950's. A state-by-state analysis of leaders who led a campaign of fear and reprisals to reduce the possibility of integration. Radical racists gained control of the councils in some states and used their voting support to win state and local elections. 397 pages with an index.

Manis, Andrew Michael. *Southern Civil Religions in Conflict: Black and White Baptists and Civil Rights, 1947-1957.* Athens: University of Georgia Press, 1987.
Describes how desegregation thwarted the ideal of a "whites only" church and society held by the largest religious denomination in the South and the United States. At the same time, it represented a fulfillment of the dream of perfection held by thousands of African American Baptists. One source of conflict and misunderstanding, many whites believed that African Americans liked segregation and wished to see it preserved. 160 pages with notes, a bibliography, and an index.

Marks, Carole. *Farewell-We're Good and Gone: The Great Migration.* Bloomington: Indiana University Press, 1989.
Finds that contrary to the prevailing view a majority of African American migrants from the South were urban, non-agricultural laborers, not the rural peasants. African Americans left the South because they were drawn to the North by higher wages, although these were still low enough to keep them in poverty. American business exploited the new arrivals just as they had been treated like mudsills in the South. 209 pages with photographs, notes, a bibliography, and an index.

Meier, August, and Elliott Rudwick. *Black Detroit and the Rise of the U.A.W.* New York: Oxford University Press, 1979.
A study of the integration of Detroit's labor force beginning with the rise of the United Auto Workers in the 1930's. African Americans first rejected unions because of the history of racism found in many older workers' organizations. Gradually, however, the union itself under Walter Reuther began to fight racism in its own ranks and finally won acceptance in the African American community.

_____, eds. *Black Protest Thought in the Twentieth Century.* Indianapolis: Bobbs-Merrill, 1971.

A useful collection of writings from W. E. B. Du Bois to Black Power advocates in the 1960's. Each selection is introduced by one of the editors and placed in its historical context. 421 pages with an index.

Moore, Jesse Thomas, Jr. *A Search for Equality: The National Urban League, 1910-1961.* University Park: Pennsylvania State University Press, 1981.
A history of a civil rights group dedicated to helping African American migrants adjust to living conditions in northern cities. The Urban League never demanded immediate, full equality but tried instead to do what was possible in terms of job training and education. 252 pages with tables and an index.

Morris, Aldon D. *The Origins of the Civil Rights Movement: Black Communities Organizing for Change.* New York: The Free Press, 1984.
A study by a sociologist of how the Civil Rights movement took root in southern communities and became a major force for change. Concentrates on the period from 1953 to 1963 with a major emphasis on churches, the NAACP, the Congress of Racial Equality (CORE), and the Student Nonviolent Coordinating Committee (SNCC). 354 pages with an index.

Nicholls, William H. *Southern Tradition and Regional Progress.* Chapel Hill: University of North Carolina Press, 1960.
A plea by a white southerner for racial tolerance. Backward thinking on race retarded education and slowed economic growth. Includes an interesting chapter on the economic aspects of school integration. 202 pages.

O'Brien, Michael. *The Idea of the American South, 1920-1941.* Baltimore: The Johns Hopkins University Press, 1979.
An intellectual history of southern identity and the people who helped create it. Chapters on Howard Odum, the sociologist; John D. Wade, a defender of agrarianism; John Ransom, the poet; literary critics Donald Davidson and Alan Tate; and historian Frank Owsley. Includes a discussion of the racial views of these southern intellectuals. 273 pages with notes and an index.

Osofsky, Gilbert. *Harlem: The Making of a Ghetto.* New York: Harper & Row, 1963.
An history of the making of America's largest racial ghetto.

Peltason, John W. *Fifty-eight Lonely Men: Southern Federal Judges and School Desegregation.* Urbana: University of Illinois Press, 1961.
Describes the role of the federal judiciary in the solution of racial problems. Relates the difficulties faced by district court judges who had to carry out the Supreme Court's *Brown* decision in the South in the 1950's. Under constant pressure to speak for the white South, some judges bowed to public pressure and delayed ordering desegregation. Others, such as Frank Johnson, Jr., were ostracized by former friends and colleagues after issuing desegregation orders in Mississippi. 288 pages with an index.

Record, Wilson. *Race and Radicalism: The NAACP and the Communist Party in Conflict.* Ithaca, N.Y.: Cornell University Press, 1964.
Covers the involvement of the two groups in many racial incidents between 1919 and 1962. The NAACP remained popular with many African Americans because it won a series of victories in court and in Congress. The Communist Party failed to attract much support because it did not deliver many results; it simply continued to call for violence and direct action. Middle-class African Americans rejected those calls. 237 pages with an index.

Reed, Linda. *Simple Decency and Common Sense: The Southern Conference Movement, 1938-1963.* Bloomington: Indiana University Press, 1991.
A study of an integrated movement of southerners who believed segregation interfered with their regions ability to build a strong economy. They called for equal opportunity in employment to help fight poverty and backwardness in their part of the country. 257 pages with a bibliographical essay, notes, and an index.

Reed, Merle E. *Seedtime for the Modern Civil Rights Movement: The President's Committee on Fair Employment Practice, 1941-1946.* Baton Rouge: Louisiana State University Press, 1991.
A study of perhaps the most controversial federal agency during World War II. Established by an executive order of the president it helped promote equal hiring practices. Hated by conservative southern senators and congressional representatives, the committee was killed by a coalition of Republicans and these conservatives from Dixie. Concludes that government can sometimes create change and improve the economic opportunity of minority groups. 384 pages with a bibliography and an index.

Ruchames, Louis. *Race, Jobs, and Politics: The Story of the FEPC.* New York: Columbia University Press, 1953.

Provides a comprehensive view of the Fair Employment Practices Commission (although it was properly titled the Commission on Fair Employment Practice). Provides a discussion of key cases and decisions involving wartime job discrimination. A history from its origins in 1941 to a filibuster by white conservatives in 1950 opposing efforts to recreate it for the Korean War. For an updated discussion, see Merle Reed's *Seedtime for the Modern Civil Rights Movement*, cited above. 255 pages with an index.

Silver, Christopher. *Twentieth Century Richmond: Planning, Politics, and Race.* Knoxville: University of Tennessee Press, 1984.

Finds that supporters of local planning used zoning to ensure continuing racial separation in the city despite a 1917 Supreme Court ruling, *Buchanan v. Warley*, that declared regulation of land uses according to race unconstitutional. Richmond's 1927 zoning ordinance contained no direct reference to race but still effectively segregated people by economic class. The use of private covenants, not declared unconstitutional until 1948, intensified racial and class separation for much of the period prior to the decision. 342 pages with a bibliographical essay and an index.

Silver, Christopher, and John V. Moeser. *The Separate City: Black Communities in the Urban South, 1940-1968.* Lexington: University Press of Kentucky, 1995.

A study of the different political cultures of Richmond, Atlanta, and Memphis. A white upper class dominated Richmond and was deeply suspicious of all lower-class residents regardless of race. Atlanta was governed by an alliance between a white corporate elite and African American business and church leaders. In Memphis, on the other hand, a working-class political machine held power in a city deeply polarized by race. Southern cities saw an increasing isolation of their African American citizens in inner-city poverty. Stable neighborhoods were collapsing in white areas and the separate black cities within the old city boundaries suffered from a continuing loss of economic power. 220 pages with tables, maps, notes, a bibliography and an index.

Singal, Daniel Joseph. *The War Within: From Victorian to Modernist Thought in the South, 1919-1945.* Chapel Hill: University of North Carolina Press, 1982.

An interesting discussion of race relations in Victorian and Modernist thought. For the Victorians, African Americans were a people without moral discipline, a race that lived by its emotions, hence truly savages. A great cultural divide separated civilization (white) from barbarism (black). White southerners rejected the modernism of contemporary authors such as William Faulkner, Robert Penn Warren, and Ellen Glasgow. They stressed the unpredictable, the disorderly, and the irrational—the same rage against the existing order found among African Americans. Hatred of blacks symbolized disgust with the evils of the modern world. Whites preferred the presumed innocence of times past. 453 pages with notes and an index.

Sitkoff, Harvard. *A New Deal for Blacks: The Emergence of Civil Rights as a National Issue.* New York: Oxford University Press, 1978.
The first of a three-volume study of the Civil Rights movement traces the development of the issues during the Great Depression. The 1930's were a time of planting seeds for future growth. The harvest would not come until the 1960's. But the faith and conviction shown by thousands of African Americans that somehow the blight of racism would one day be erased never wavered. The Roosevelt Administration helped by providing relief and employment for innumerable people. 397 pages with notes and an index.

Sitkoff, Harvard. *The Struggle for Black Equality, 1954-1980.* New York: Hill & Wang, 1981.
The final volume in Sitkoff's trilogy tracing the history of race relations in the United States since the Great Depression.

Sochen, June, ed. *The Black Man and the American Dream: Negro Aspirations in America, 1900-1930.* Chicago: Quadrangle Books, 1971.
A collection of documents, essays, and newspaper article on various subjects including politics, education, equality, economics, race relations, and separatism. Each chapter is ably introduced by the editor. 372 pages.

Tauber, Karl E., and Alma K. Tauber. *Negroes in Cities: Residential Segregation and Neighborhood Change.* Chicago: University of Chicago Press, 1965.
Uses census data to trace the growth of Chicago's black communities. A work of demography and sociology with only a bit of historical background. Finds racism rampant in white neighborhoods. 474 pages with tables, maps, and an index.

Trotter, Joe William, Jr., ed. *The Great Migration in Historical Perspective: New Dimensions of Race, Class, and Gender.* Bloomington: Indiana University Press, 1991.

A brief series of eight essays on migrations into and out of Norfolk, Pittsburgh, Chicago, Richmond, Los Angeles, and southern West Virginia. Finds that black migration to the North was often preceded by a series of stops in a southern small city or town. Most migrants did not come north directly from rural areas. 160 pages with notes and an index.

Vose, Clement E. *Caucasians Only: The Supreme Court, The NAACP and the Restrictive Covenant Cases.* Rev. ed. Berkeley: University of California Press, 1967.

Originally published in 1959, Vose's work describes the sociological and political events leading to the Supreme Court's 1948 decision outlawing private contracts preventing a sale of property because of a buyer's race. Also has a discussion of the legal tactics adopted by the NAACP in order to win this major case. 296 pages with pictures and an index.

Weiss, Nancy. *Farewell to the Party of Lincoln: Black Politics in the Age of FDR.* Princeton, N.J.: Princeton University Press, 1983.

Explains how the New Deal and the Great Depression moved African American voters into a new party, the Democrats. Also a discussion of the many jobs and programs the New Deal made available to African Americans for the first time.

_____. *The National Urban League, 1910-1940,* New York: Oxford University Press, 1974.

A history of a civil rights group dedicated to education and job training. Describes how it came into being and the influence it had mainly in northern cities.

Whitman, Mark, ed. *Removing a Badge of Slavery: The Record of Brown v. Board of Education.* Princeton, N.J.: Marcus Wiener, 1993.

Contains the full legal record of the case with introductions and annotations by the editor. Includes *Plessy v. Ferguson* and briefs, oral arguments, and legal articles pertaining to the *Brown* case. 357 pages.

Wilson, James Q. *Negro Politics: The Search for Leadership.* Glencoe, Ill.: The Free Press, 1960.

A political scientist views African American society and finds a shortage of qualified leaders. Describes the significant influence of gamblers and gang leaders in black neighborhoods. Based on research done in Chicago in the 1950's.

Wolters, Raymond. *Negroes and the Great Depression.* Westport, Conn.: Greenwood Press, 1970.
An analysis of the way African Americans were effected by New Deal social programs. Leaders of many New Deal agencies did not have the will to make changes necessary to achieve racial justice. Most programs did not help blacks; benefits did not trickle down to the sharecroppers and the poor as was expected. Most aid helped wealthier and less economically troubled Americans. 398 pages with an index.

Wynn, Neil A. *The Afro-American and the Second World War.* New York: Holmes & Meier, 1976. Rev. ed. New York: Holmes & Meier, 1993.
A well-written general survey of African Americans in the military and in civilian life. Describes the effects of segregation, prejudice, race riots, and discrimination. Also surveys the achievements and accomplishments of black soldiers and sailors under very trying circumstances.

Chapter 10

CIVIL RIGHTS AND RACE, 1961-1995

Ball, Howard, Dale Krane, and Thomas P. Lauth, eds. *Compromised Compliance: Implementation of the 1965 Voting Rights Act.* Westport, Conn.: Greenwood Press, 1982.
Essays on federal enforcement of the law and the limits of federal intervention.

Banner-Haley, Charles T. *The Fruits of Integration: Black Middle-Class Ideology and Culture, 1960-1990.* Jackson: University Press of Mississippi, 1994.
Raises questions about the development of ideology and culture during a period of rising affluence for a key part of the African American community. Describes the debate over integration versus nationalism and discusses the image of African Americans in television, motion pictures, popular music, and art. Finds a great diversity of opinions and views within the middle class. 232 pages with a select bibliography, notes, and an index.

Barkun, Michael. *Religion and the Racist Right: The Origins of the Christian Identity Movement.* Chapel Hill: University of North Carolina Press, 1994.
A survey of the origins, literature, and leading figures and ideas of the movement. The world is on the verge of an apocalyptic struggle between whites (Aryans) and a Jewish conspiracy that includes pre-humans (African American). Jews are the children of Satan and Eve. Whites are here to do God's work and are the true Children of Israel. A vivid description of these bizarre ideas. 290 pages with an index

Bartley, Numan V. *The New South: 1945-1980.* Baton Rouge: Louisiana State University Press, 1995.
A distinguished volume in the History of the South series. Three key chapters on race relations include "Race and Reform" (chapter 5), "Race and Reaction" (chapter 6), and "The Civil Rights Movement" (chapter 9). 547 pages, including a critical essay on sources and an index.

Beardslee, William R. *The Way Out Must Lead in: Life Histories in the Civil Rights Movement.* Atlanta: Center for Research in Social Change, Emory University, 1977.
Interviews of civil rights leaders by a physician and psychiatrist who was also an activist. Includes the views of John Lewis, Annie Williams, a black sheriff in Alabama, and a black minister. They discuss what they gained and lost in the movement and how racism affected their lives. 169 pages.

Beifuss, Joan Turner. *At the River I Stand: Memphis, the 1968 Strike, and Martin Luther King.* Brooklyn, N.Y.: Carlson Publishing, 1989.
Based on 364 interviews made during and after the strike of sanitation workers who participated in the strike. This volume, the twelfth in Carlson's *Martin Luther King, Jr., and the Civil Rights Movement* series, includes transcripts of the taped interviews, other documents, and a history of the strike. 370 pages with and index.

Berman, Paul, ed. *Blacks and Jews: Alliances and Arguments.* New York: Delacorte Press, 1994.
A collection of essays by James Baldwin, Clayborne Carson, Andrew Hacker, Shelby Steele, and others on relations between African Americans and Jews since the 1960's. Includes a essay on the rioting in Crown Heights in 1991, the Leonard Jeffries affair at the City University of New York, and a discussion of the Nation of Islam and its anti-Semitic beliefs. 303 pages.

Black, Earl. *Southern Governors and Civil Rights: Racial Segregation as a Campaign Issue in the Second Reconstruction.* Cambridge, Mass.: Harvard University Press, 1976.
A case study of a white elite in the South from 1954 to 1973. Describes the impact of the federal government on political campaigning. Those candidates who showed the most sympathy toward African American demands were always defeated. Because of pressure from Washington, however, segregation was not reinstated. Race remained the key issue in most campaigns. 408 pages with tables, figures, and an index.

Blair, Thomas L. *Retreat to the Ghetto: The End of a Dream?* New York: Hill & Wang, 1977.
Examines the black separatism of Malcolm X and the Black Power movement of the late 1960's. "Ethnic pluralism" was nothing but a new name for segregation and separatism, the author concludes. 263 pages.

Blalock, Hubert M., Jr. *Black-White Relations in the 1980's: Toward a Long-Term Policy.* New York: Praeger, 1985.
A series of recommendations by a sociologist on how the improve race relations through job training and education programs. Calls for a long-range series of programs and policies that would help reduce racial antagonism. 208 pages.

Boles, John B., ed. *Dixie Dateline: A Journalistic Portrait of the Contemporary South.* Houston, Tex.: Rice University Press, 1983.
A collection of essays by journalists and historians on race relations in the late 1970's. Finds the Civil Rights movement in complete disarray and virtually leaderless. Paul Delaney's "A New South for Blacks?" has some useful insights.

Blumberg, Rhoda Lois. *Civil Rights: The 1960's Freedom Struggle.* Boston: Twayne, 1991.
A history of the movement by a sociologist that is readable and brief. Includes a brief review of race relations in the United States. Chapters on the Montgomery Bus Boycott, sit-ins, freedom rides, the campaign for voting rights, the Black Power movement, the northern race riots, and the decline of the movement after the assassination of Martin Luther King, Jr. 244 pages with photographs and an index.

Brauer, Carl M. *John F. Kennedy and the Second Reconstruction.* New York: Columbia University Press, 1977.
Describes and evaluates President Kennedy's role in trying to move beyond racial politics by stressing equal economic opportunity. Examines the major political difficulties the administration faced because of Republican-Conservative Democrat opposition to any social or economic reform. Finds that Kennedy supported a vigorous and far-reaching effort to eliminate racial discrimination from the United States. Congressional opposition, however, stymied such efforts. 396 pages with notes and an index.

Brink, William, and Louis Harris. *The Negro Revolution in America.* New York: Simon & Schuster, 1963.
A series of tables and analyses based on a nationwide survey published in *Newsweek* in July and October of 1963. Chapters on what the African American community wanted; why and how they supported the sit-ins and voting rights movement; which political candidates they supported, and what white Americans thought of the movement and its demands. 249 pages with tables and an index.

Brooks, Thomas R. *Walls Came Tumbling Down: A History of the Civil Rights Movement, 1940-1970.* Englewood Cliffs, N.J.: Prentice-Hall, 1974.
A early, brief history of the movement with interesting portraits of leaders and opponents of equal rights.

Browning, Rufus P., Dale Rogers Marshall, and David H. Tabb. *Protest Is Not Enough: The Struggle of Blacks and Hispanics for Equality in Urban Politics.* Berkeley: University of California Press, 1984.
A study of ten California cities and their efforts to increase minority representation and participation. Explores how a variety of policies and approaches were implemented and how they did manage to involve larger numbers of African Americans and Hispanics in the political process. 317 pages with tables and an index.

Button, James W. *Blacks and Social Change: Impact of the Civil Rights Movement in Southern Communities.* Princeton, N.J.: Princeton University Press, 1989.
A study based on surveys and interviews in Florida over a fifteen-year period. Protests and even violence often proved necessary to produce any change in race relations. Conventional political involvement and debate most often led to limited, slow changes. Still, the 1960's and 1970's brought more changes to African Americans than ever before, at least in terms of controlling their own destiny. 326 pages with tables and an index.

Carson, Clayborne. *In Struggle: SNCC and the Black Awakening of the 1960's.* Cambridge, Mass.: Harvard University Press, 1981.
A description of the origins and impact of the Student Nonviolent Coordinating Committee. An intellectual history based on interviews with members, transcripts of meetings, documents, and eyewitness accounts of this very important group. Includes an analysis of the many arguments over tactics, Black Power philosophy, and the goals of the members. 359 pages with an index.

Carson, Clayborne, et al., eds. *Eyes on the Prize: America's Civil Rights Years: A Reader and Guide.* New York: Penguin Books, 1987.
Prepared as a guide to accompany the excellent television documentary of the same name, this work contains many writings, documents, and photographs relating to the birth, success, and decline of the movement.

Chafe, William. *Civilities and Civil Rights: Greensboro, North Carolina, and the Black Struggle for Freedom.* New York: Oxford University Press, 1980.

A history of the movement in the city where sit-ins began by a major historian of twentieth century American society. Describes how and why they began here and how they grew and spread throughout the South. Explores the heritage of African American protest leading up to the sit-ins and how the white community sought to contain the protests. The movement represented the best hope for American society. 436 pages with notes and an index.

Chappell, David L. *Inside Agitators: White Southerners in the Civil Rights Movement.* Baltimore: The Johns Hopkins University Press, 1994.

Concerned with the relationship between morality and politics, the author, a historian, describes of importance of a small group of white sympathizers to the growth of the movement. African American leaders took advantage of this white sympathy and also knew how to exploit the divisions among segregationists. Above all, the movement benefited from remembering King's point about hating the sin and loving the sinner. 293 pages with a bibliographic essay, notes, and an index.

Clark, E. Culpepper. *The Schoolhouse Door: Segregation's Last Stand at the University of Alabama.* New York: Oxford University Press, 1993.

The confrontation between Governor George Wallace at President Kennedy cost the Democrats the South in the 1962 election. Kennedy took action to protect two black students enrolled at the University of Alabama and forced the governor to step aside. Only federal government action made the university register the students. Had it not acted it would have remained totally white. 305 pages with photographs, a bibliography, and an index.

Couto, Richard A. *Ain't Gonna Let Nobody Turn Me Round: The Pursuit of Racial Justice in the Rural South.* Philadelphia: Temple University Press, 1991.

A study of race relations in Haywood, Tennessee; Lee County, Arkansas; Lowndes County, Alabama, and the Sea Islands of South Carolina. Based on interviews with residents, it traces the history of black-white relations back into the 1930's. Presents an evaluation of the New Deal programs and the War on Poverty of the 1960's. Although both reform movements improved the quality of life for many, they did not go far enough to reduce terrible poverty. An interesting and provocative study. 421 pages with notes and an index.

Davidson, Chandler, ed. *Minority Vote Dilution.* Washington, D.C.: Brookings Institution Press, 1984.

A series of essays that study the impact of the Voting Rights Act of 1965 as amended in 1982 to promote the creation of minority voting districts. A key essay by Milton D. Morris, "Black Electoral Participation and the Distribution of Public Benefits," finds that the increase in African American voting power after 1965 had little effect on public policy. Most legislative districts remained firmly under the control of whites because of racial gerrymandering.

Dittmer, John. *Local People: The Struggle for Civil Rights in Mississippi.* Urbana: University of Illinois Press, 1994.

Reviews changes that took place in the 1960's and 1970's. At first, white intimidation kept African Americans from voting in local and state elections. The influence of the Citizens Councils and the Ku Klux Klan made a mockery of the law. As voting registration increased among blacks, and it reached 60 percent by 1968 almost equal to that of whites, the use of terror declined. Political participation did not lead to improved economic circumstances for African Americans. Impoverished blacks were largely forgotten by white politicians, and their income remained less than half of the white majority. 530 pages with notes and an index.

Drake, St. Clair. *Race Relations in a Time of Rapid Social Change.* New York: National Federation of Settlements and Neighborhood Centers, 1966.

A history of settlement houses and their involvement with race relations by a distinguished sociologist. Includes a survey of staff attitudes and of the views of boards of directors. Asks whether liberals working in settlements really understand African American feelings. 168 pages.

Draper, Alan. *Conflict of Interests: Organized Labor and the Civil Rights Movement in the South, 1954-1968.* Ithaca, N.Y.: ILR Press, 1994.

Records some fundamental changes in attitudes. Before 1964, white workers gave the Democratic Party credit and felt gratitude toward it because of its efforts in labor's behalf. By the 1970's, they resented the party and blamed it for taking too much from their paychecks to finance "welfare." White workers see themselves as victims of a system rewarding non-working minorities. An important book on a little discussed topic. 234 pages with notes, a bibliography, and an index.

Draper, Theodore. *The Rediscovery of Black Nationalism.* New York: Viking Press, 1970.

A history of the Black Panther Party from 1965 to 1969. Includes a discussion of other twentieth century nationalist groups, including Marcus Garvey and Elijah Muhammad. Suggests that black nationalism becomes popular during times of despair and lack of progress in improving race relations.

Eagles, Charles W., ed. *The Civil Rights Movement in America.* Jackson: University Press of Mississippi, 1986.
Historical essays chiefly concerned with the campaign for voting rights in Mississippi. John Dittmer's "The Politics of the Mississippi Movement, 1954-64" is especially informative about the Mississippi Freedom Democratic Party of 1964.

Fairclough, Adam. *"To Redeem the Soul of America": The SCLC and Martin Luther King, Jr.* Athens: University of Georgia Press, 1987.
Describes the organization and growth of the Southern Christian Leadership Conference under the guidance of King. African Americans confronted a very difficult problem, how to secure equal rights under the law from a racist white majority. The solution was to appeal to federal power. The SCLC carried out this policy very well by gaining the spotlight in a number of key areas and winning the support of many white Christians in the North. 504 pages with illustrations and an index.

Freyer, Tony. *The Little Rock Crisis: A Constitutional Interpretation.* Westport, Conn.: Greenwood Press, 1984.
Presents the legal context of the *Brown* decision and places it into the social culture of the white South. In Little Rock in 1957, federal government action demonstrated that judicial lawmaking could eventually force public acceptance of desegregation. Small changes took place in the school system that slowly helped change views of race. It took a long time and some violence but racial justice finally triumphed over conservative principles of inequality. 186 pages with an index.

Fullinwider, S. P. *The Mind and Mood of Black America: Twentieth Century Thought.* Homewood, Ill.: Dorsey Press, 1969.
A study in the history of ideas regarding race, inferiority, and identity. Oppression robbed African Americans of status which some sought to win back by asserting moral superiority or by turning aggressive. Describes the mystical community of "soul brothers" who were more loving, moral, and humane than the white man. The mythical African American had more love for feeling, as in his music, than did coldly rationalistic whites. Includes an interesting discussion of African American literature, poetry, and music. 255 pages with an index.

Garrow, David J. *Bearing the Cross: Martin Luther King, Jr., and the Southern Christian Leadership Conference.* New York: Alfred A. Knopf, 1986.
Stresses the religious aspects of the crusade for voting and civil rights. King is portrayed as heroic, yet filled with doubt, guilt, and loneliness.

_____. *Protest at Selma: Martin Luther King, Jr., and the Voting Rights Act of 1965.* New Haven, Conn.: Yale University Press, 1978.
Provides a discussion of the relationship between protest and politics.

_____, ed. *We Shall Overcome: The Civil Rights Movement in the United States in the 1950's and 1960's.* 3 vols. Brooklyn, N.Y.: Carlson Publishing, 1989.

_____, ed. *The Walking City: The Montgomery Bus Boycott, 1955-1956.* Brooklyn, N.Y.: Carlson Publishing, 1989.

_____, ed. *Birmingham, Alabama, 1956-1963: The Black Struggle for Civil Rights.* Brooklyn, N.Y.: Carlson Publishing, 1989.

_____, ed. *Atlanta, Georgia, 1960-1961: Sit-Ins and Student Activism.* Brooklyn, N.Y.: Carlson Publishing, 1989.

_____, ed. *St. Augustine, Florida, 1963-1964: Mass Protest and Racial Violence.* Brooklyn, N.Y.: Carlson Publishing, 1989.

_____, ed. *Chicago 1966: Open Housing Marches, Summit Negotiations, and Operation Breadbasket.* Brooklyn, N.Y.: Carlson Publishing, 1989.
Edited and introduced by Garrow, these are among the projected eighteen volumes of the series *Martin Luther King, Jr., and the Civil Rights Movement,* which brings together key unpublished material and significant books and articles previously published. Undoubtedly this will be the most important resource for future scholars interested in King's life and works. Other titles in this series are listed by individual author.

Golden, Marita, and Susan Richards Shreve, eds. *Skin Deep: Black Women and White Women Write About Race.* New York: Doubleday, 1995.
Twenty essays and works of fiction. Mostly unpublished material from authors such as Joyce Carol Oates, bell hooks, Toni Morrison, and Alice Walker. 309 pages.

Goldman, Peter. *Report from Black America*. New York: Simon & Schuster, 1969.
A discussion based on Gallup polls conducted between 1963 and 1969. The polling data and questions appear in an appendix. Goldman draws the key conclusion that there are two Americas, alien and separate and growing more so over time. 282 pages with an index.

Graglia, Lino A. *Disaster by Decree: The Supreme Court Decisions on Race and the Schools*. Ithaca, N.Y.: Cornell University Press, 1976.
A negative view of busing. Suggests that compulsory racial integration, and all such attempts to teach children the irrelevance of race, can be quickly undone. Racial hatred was only increased by busing in the school districts studied. 351 pages with an index.

Graham, Hugh Davis. *The Civil Rights Era: Origins and Development of National Policy, 1960-1972*. New York: Oxford University Press, 1990.
Describes the development and radical shift in policy that took place in the 1960's. Includes an analysis of the 1964, 1965, 1968, and 1972 civil rights laws and key court decisions interpreting those laws. Federal policy broke the back of legal segregation under Kennedy and Johnson. Nixon began a reversal of racial policies which helped the growth of the Republican Party in the South. 578 pages with notes and an index.

Haines, Herbert H. *Black Radicals and the Civil Rights Mainstream, 1954-1970*. Knoxville: University of Tennessee Press, 1988.
The role of militant groups in the Civil Rights movement and how they tried to influence moderates. Includes brief histories of the Congress of Racial Equality (CORE), the Student Nonviolent Coordinating Committee (SNCC), the Black Panther Party, and the Marxist-Leninist Revolutionary Action Movement (RAM). 231 pages with an index.

Hall, Raymond L. *Black Separatism in the United States*. Hanover, N.H.: University Press of New England, 1978.
A study of the Nation of Islam, Congress of Racial Equality (CORE), the Black Panthers, and the Republic of New Afrika. Concludes that members of these groups had given up on America and were seeking places where they could control their own destiny. 306 pages with notes and an index.

Holloway, Karla F. C. *Codes of Conduct: Race, Ethics, and the Color of Our Character*. New Brunswick, N.J.: Rutgers University Press, 1995.

A series of "meditations" on black women and the visual power of the black female body, among other things. A somewhat strange work of scholarship. 225 pages with an index.

Horton, Aimee Isgrig. *The Highlander Folk School: A History of Its Major Programs, 1932-1961.* Brooklyn, N.Y.: Carlson Publishing, 1989.
Volume 13 in the *Martin Luther King, Jr.* series edited by David Garrow. Describes the importance of this "school" of race relations in eastern Tennessee. Many important civil rights leaders attended seminars and discussions at Miles Horton's academy in the 1940's and 1950's.

Inger, Morton. *Politics and Reality in an American City: The New Orleans School Crisis of 1960.* New York: Center for Urban Education, 1969.
Analyzes an early white boycott of public schools under federal court orders to desegregate. Most whites in the city supported the boycott and began sending their children to private segregated schools.

Jacoway, Elizabeth, and David R. Colburn, eds. *Southern Businessmen and Desegregation.* Baton Rouge: Louisiana State University Press, 1982.
Essays that refute the myth that business leaders took the lead in pushing for integration. Only the combination of African American pressure and the image-consciousness of political leaders—it looked bad for whites to be beating up on blacks—moved the business community to action. Has essays concerning desegregation in New Orleans, Atlanta, Little Rock, and Norfolk. 292 pages with an index.

Jennings, James, ed. *Race, Politics and Economic Development: Community Perspectives.* London: Verso Publishers, 1992.
Eleven essays by Marxist scholars on the emergence of the underclass and the crisis of black youth. Surveys urban and racial policies in the United States in the 1980's. Contains a call for action to reverse policies harmful to African Americans. 189 pages with an index.

Keesing's Research Report. *Race Relations in the USA: 1954-1968.* New York: Charles Scribner's Sons, 1970.
A vast compilation of statistics and facts concerning the impact of the Civil Rights movement after the *Brown* decision. 280 pages with an index.

Killian, Lewis, and Charles Grigg. *Racial Crisis in America: Leadership in Conflict.* Englewood Cliffs, N.J.: Prentice-Hall, 1964.

A early warning about the possibility of conflict in the future. Describes African American leadership in the South. Based on interviews and opinion polling. Explains the almost impossible task for leaders, any reform they called for required some loss to whites, in terms of economics or prestige. Sees little reason for hope. 144 pages with an index.

Klibaner, Irwin. *Conscience of a Troubled South: The Southern Conference Educational Fund, 1946-1966.* Brooklyn, N.Y.: Carlson Publishing, 1989.
Volume 14 in the *Martin Luther King, Jr.* series edited by David Garrow. Klibaner has written a history of a small, but important interracial group committed to improving education and race relations in the South.

Laue, James H. *Direct Action and Desegregation, 1960-1962: Toward a Theory of the Rationalization of Protest.* Brooklyn, N.Y.: Carlson Publishing, 1989.
Volume 15 in the *Martin Luther King, Jr.* series edited by David Garrow. A history of the early days of the Student Nonviolent Coordinating Committee and its discussions about tactics, ethics, and political protest.

Lawson, Steven F. *In Pursuit of Power: Southern Blacks and Electoral Politics, 1965-1982.* New York: Columbia University Press, 1985.
A continuation of the author's previous work on African American politics in the South, *Black Ballots.* Race was still a major factor during this time. Voting rights had been won, but a quick withdrawal of federal government supervision of elections caused great harm in the 1970's. Vigilance over voting registrars and enemies of racial equality remained necessary but was not provided. Voting rights did little to improve African American economic advance—the future in that area continued to look very bleak. 391 pages with notes and an index.

Levy, Peter B., ed. *Documentary History of the Modern Civil Rights Movement.* New York: Greenwood Press, 1992.
Contains documents from the early 1940's to the latter days of the Student Nonviolent Coordinating Committee (SNCC) and the Students for a Democratic Society (SDS). Includes prose, poetry, statistics, and documents from the "white resistance." 275 pages with an index.

Lincoln, C. Eric. *Race, Religion, and the Continuing American Dilemma.* New York: Hill & Wang, 1984.

A history of white and African American religions. Describes views of race relations, equality, and justice.

Loevy, Robert D. *To End All Segregation: The Politics of the Passage of the Civil Rights Act of 1964.* Lanham, Md.: University Press of America, 1990.
A legislative history by a political scientist and former assistant to Republican Senator Thomas Kuchel, a key supporter of the bill. A detailed account of the eighty-three-day debate that took up more than 6,300 pages in the *Congressional Record.* Gives much credit for the bill's final passage to Senator Everett Dirksen, a Republican from Illinois. His was the key vote ending the southern filibuster. Follows the legislation from introduction to final passage. 373 pages with an index.

Marable, Manning. *Race, Reform, and Rebellion: The Second Reconstruction in Black America, 1945-1990.* Jackson: University Press of Mississippi, 1991.
Written by a leading black scholar with a Marxist perspective, this work surveys the politics and tactics of the Civil Rights movement. Marable describes the influence of the protest movements, African American leaders, political parties, government policy makers, and corporate America in supporting and opposing equality of rights. Despite political gains, poverty and discrimination remained major problems in the lives of many African Americans. Marable criticizes the Second Reconstruction for failing to provide employment, health care, or good schools. 283 pages with notes and an index.

Matthews, Donald R., and James W. Prothro. *Negroes and the New Southern Politics.* New York: Columbia University Press, 1966.
A study of the impact of the Voting Rights Act of 1965 on African American political participation by two political scientists. Many graphs and charts show the tremendous growth in registration, voting, and election of blacks in the South to office. 472 pages with an index.

Miller, Kent S., and Ralph Mason Dreger. *Comparative Studies of Blacks and Whites in the United States.* New York: Seminar Press, 1973.
Includes significant original essays written by psychologists and sociologists. Describes research in a variety of fields, including language usage, the effects of education, the effects of school desegregation, and the mental health of African Americans. 572 pages with an index.

Morris, Aldon D. *The Origins of the Civil Rights Movement: Black Communities Organizing for Change.* New York: Free Press, 1984.
Chiefly about the impact of Martin Luther King, Jr., and the role of the Southern Christian Leadership Conference in bringing together various African American groups in southern communities.

Moses, Wilson Jeremiah. *Black Messiahs and Uncle Toms: Social and Literary Manipulators of a Religious Myth.* University Park: Pennsylvania State University Press, 1982.
Sees "Uncle Tom" as a symbol of misguided love and altruism. Presents a literary interpretation and history of the writings of Booker T. Washington, Marcus Garvey, W. E. B. Du Bois, and Malcolm X. Includes an index.

Muse, Benjamin. *The American Negro Revolution: From Nonviolence to Black Power, 1963-1967.* Bloomington: Indiana University Press, 1968.
From the March on Washington to the Kerner Report, a leading African American historian presents a well-written survey of the problems, trends, and events that took place during this dramatic period of change. 345 pages with an index.

_____. *The Years of Prelude: The Story of Integration Since the Supreme Court's 1954 Decision.* New York: Viking Press, 1964.
Describes the Eisenhower record on civil rights and the importance of the *Brown* decision. 308 pages with an index.

Namorato, Michael V., ed. *Have We Overcome?: Race Relations Since Brown: Essays.* Jackson: University Press of Mississippi, 1979.
A series of essays from a symposium on the topic. The papers conclude that their still is a long way to go before the question in the title can be answered positively, but a beginning has been made.

Neilson, Melany. *Even Mississippi.* Tuscaloosa: University of Alabama Press, 1989.
The story of a white woman who worked in the congressional campaigns of Robert Clark, a African American who ran an lost twice (1980 and 1982) to a white Republican. 199 pages.

Norrell, Robert J. *Reaping the Whirlwind: The Civil Rights Movement in Tuskegee.* New York: Alfred A. Knopf, 1985.
Details the efforts made by African Americans in Booker T. Washington's hometown to gain the right to vote, and how whites resisted and

kept control. Two communities, separate and unequal emerged. 254 pages with notes, photos, and an index.

Oppenheimer, Martin. *The Sit-In Movement of 1960.* Brooklyn, N.Y.: Carlson Publishing, 1989.
Volume 16 in the *Martin Luther King, Jr.* series edited by David Garrow. Originally published in 1963, this is a study by a sociologist of several different communities and their response to the first sit-ins. Includes an analysis of events in Nashville, Tennessee; Atlanta, Georgia; Jacksonville and Tallahassee, Florida; and Columbia, Rock Hill, and Orangeburg, South Carolina; and Lawrenceville, Virginia. 222 pages with notes and an index.

Panetta, Leon E., and Peter Gall. *Bring Us Together: The Nixon Team and the Civil Rights Retreat.* Philadelphia: J. B. Lippincott, 1971.
Panetta, who later became President Clinton's chief White House assistant, writes about his experience as director of civil rights in the Department of Health, Education, and Welfare in 1969 and 1970. He resigned that position in February of 1970. President Richard Nixon actively sought out the worst elements in the Deep South as part of his "southern strategy" in the 1968 election and rewarded their support with a major campaign against enforcing civil rights laws. 380 pages with an index.

Peake, Thomas R. *Keeping the Dream Alive: A History of the Southern Christian Leadership Conference from King to the Nineteen-Eighties.* New York: Peter Lang, 1987.
A general history that stresses King's role and legacy. Based on interviews with members and leaders, it also has much information about the leadership of Ralph David Abernathy, president from 1968 to 1977, and his successor, Joseph Lowery. 492 pages with notes and an index.

Phillips, William M., Jr. *An Unillustrious Alliance: The African American and Jewish American Communities.* New York: Greenwood Press, 1991.
An African American sociologist explores the relationship between two minorities. Both have experienced histories of prejudice and discrimination. Both have been subjected to bigotry, exclusion, and rejection. Yet the two groups have had a difficult and stormy relationship. Similar experiences of racism had not bred a spirit of understanding, though most prejudice for these groups came from the

African American community rather than the Jewish. 162 pages with an index.

Pride, Richard A., and J. David Woodard. *The Burden of Busing: The Politics of Desegregation in Nashville, Tennessee.* Knoxville: University of Tennessee Press, 1985.
Describes efforts in Nashville to support and oppose court-ordered desegregation. Studies the attitudes of both sides in the 1970's and how they changed over time. 302 pages with illustrations, tables, and an index.

Raines, Howell. *My Soul Is Rested: Movement Days in the Deep South Remembered.* New York: G. P. Putnam's Sons, 1977.
An oral history of the movement in Montgomery and Selma, Alabama, and other key areas of confrontation. Interviews with participants on both sides are included. 472 pages.

Roberts, Ronald S. *Clarence Thomas and the Tough Love Crowd: Counterfeit Heroes and Unhappy Truths.* New York: New York University Press, 1995.
A critique of neoconservative blacks such as Clarence Thomas, Shelby Steele, Stephen L. Carter, and others who reject affirmative action. 221 pages.

Rothschild, Mary Aickin. *A Case of Black and White: Northern Volunteers and the Southern Freedom Summers, 1964-1965.* Westport, Conn.: Greenwood Press, 1982.
Rothschild finds that most white volunteers had no idea of what they were committing themselves to in the South. The intensity of the racism of whites in the South surprised these northerners. These northern members of the Student Nonviolent Coordinating Committee (SNCC), Students for a Democratic Society (SDS) and other groups were courageous, generous, and hardworking agents of change. 213 pages with an index.

Salter, John R. *Jackson, Mississippi: An American Chronicle of Struggle and Schism.* Hicksville, N.Y.: Exposition Press, 1979. Reprint. Malabar, Fla.: R. E. Krieger, 1987.
A profile of Medgar Evers and the NAACP from its early days to the crisis the group experienced after his murder.

Schwartz, Bernard. *Swann's Way: The School Busing Case and the Supreme Court.* New York: Oxford University Press, 1986.

An oral and documentary history based on interviews with Supreme Court justices, law clerks, and the attorneys involved in the key decision. 245 pages with notes and an index.

Silberman, Charles. *Crisis in Black and White.* New York: Random House, 1964.
A study of the crisis in inner-city schools by a journalist. One of the first works to address problems in northern schools.

Small, Stephen. *Racialized Barriers: The Black Experience in the United States and England in the 1980s.* London: Routledge, 1994.
A survey and comparison of oppression and discrimination in both countries. Includes a description of the significance of social class and income on treatment accorded to group members. 247 pages with an index.

Stoper, Emily. *The Student Nonviolent Coordinating Committee: The Growth of Radicalism in a Civil Rights Organization.* Brooklyn, N.Y.: Carlson Publishing, 1989.
Volume 17 in the *Martin Luther King, Jr.* series edited by David Garrow. A history of this group from 1963 to 1968. Describes key issues and debates over black power in the group.

Thomas, Gail E., ed. *U.S. Race Relations in the 1980's and 1990's: Challenges and Alternatives.* New York: Hemisphere, 1990.
Twenty essays by social scientists on topics ranging from "Education and Race" to "Occupational Mobility, Economics, and Cultural Pluralism." First presented at a conference on race and ethnic relations at Texas A&M University in conjunction with the twentieth anniversary of the Kerner Report. 281 pages with an index.

Vander Zanden, James W. *Race Relations in Transition: The Segregation Crisis in the South.* New York: Random House, 1965.
A sociologist surveys the stresses and strains to the social structure produced by the Civil Rights movement. Describes the rise of White Citizens Councils, the Ku Klux Klan, and other supremacist groups. 135 pages with an index.

Wexler, Sanford. *The Civil Rights Movement: An Eyewitness History.* New York: Facts On File, 1993.
A documentary history of the movement since 1954 with many photographs, biographies, and key sources. Includes congressional debates,

newspaper editorials, speeches, and songs. 368 pages with notes and an index.

Willie, Charles V., ed. *Black/Brown/White Relations: Race Relations in the 1970's.* New Brunswick, N.J.: Transaction Books, 1977.
Thirteen essays by a leading student of American race relations, most previously published in *Transaction/Society Magazine.* Emphasizes the institutional sources and support for racism and prejudice. 235 pages with an index.

Wirt, Frederick M. *Politics of Southern Equality: Law and Social Change in a Mississippi County.* Chicago: Aldine Publishing, 1970.
A study of Panola County and its demographic, economic, and political background. Describes what actually changed as a result of civil rights activity. Efforts to claim that the law could not change beliefs, and that morality could not be enforced through law, proved wrong. Had outside pressure not been mobilized local racial attitudes and behavior would not have changed. 335 pages with an index.

Wolters, Raymond. *The Burden of Brown: Thirty Years of School Deseg-regation.* Knoxville: University of Tennessee Press, 1984.
Describes how things have worked out and an analysis of the decision. The Supreme Court's major premise was that official segregation was a denial of equal protection under the law. Its minor premise was that racial discrimination damaged the confidence of African American children and distorted their self-image. Finds much that is discouraging about what happened to public schools after the *Brown* decision. Especially critical of effort to bus students to create racial parity. All that the Constitution required, in the author's view, was that each person be treated as an individual without regard to race. 346 pages with tables and an index.

Chapter 11

THE COSTS OF PREJUDICE AND DISCRIMINATION

Allport, Gordon. *The Nature of Prejudice.* Cambridge, Mass.: Harvard University Press, 1954.
The classic psychological account of the development of prejudice in individuals. Useful for understanding the origins of racial hatred and the personalities of those individuals who have learned how to hate. An interesting antidote to those analyses based solely on social structures and "institutional" racism.

America, Richard F. *The Wealth of Races: The Present Value of Benefits from Past Injustices.* New York: Greenwood Press, 1990.
An amazing book from the National Economic Association, the professional association of African American economists. It sheds light on the extent of benefits that large numbers of Americans are currently realizing from past economic relationships which caused great damage to many other people. Finds that racial discrimination, exclusion, and exploitation in employment, education, and housing, have given white Americans at least a 30 percent advantage in income over their black neighbors. This is the economic case for affirmative action. 219 pages with a select bibliography and an index.

Apostle, Richard A., et al. *The Anatomy of Racial Attitudes.* Berkeley: University of California Press, 1983.
Based on a survey of two thousand people in California. Its key conclusions on white attitudes: 17 percent of whites believe that blacks are innately inferior to whites and that it is perfectly natural that blacks are underprivileged; 39 percent blame blacks for being lazy. "If only they would work hard enough" they would get ahead; 22 percent believe the different levels of economic success in America are a result of God's intentions, He ordained the races to be different and whites are really his chosen people; 18 percent accept the view that black economic inequality results from a hostile environment, while the remaining 4 percent settle simply on "racism" as the cause. Results such as these do not inspire great hope for major changes in attitudes or structure in the future. 342 pages with and index.

Banner-Haley, Charles T. *The Fruits of Integration: Black Middle-Class Ideology and Culture, 1960-1990.* Jackson: University Press of Mississippi, 1994.

Examines the evolution and influence of the educated "black bourgeoisie" on the racial climate. Discusses class distinctions, with the black middle class still associated by color with African Americans in poverty, whether they want to be or not. Also describes how the color line still haunts the lives of all African Americans no matter how successful. Analyzes the debate between integrationists and nationalists raising key questions about the shortcomings of both points of view. 232 pages with notes, a select bibliography, and an index.

Banton, Michael. *Discrimination.* Philadelphia: Open University Press, 1994.

A slender but thoughtful little volume on the idea of discrimination. Is it ever right? Is making it against the law the best and most effective method of fighting it? Traces the history of discrimination based on gender and race. 103 pages with and index.

Bowser, Benjamin P., and Raymond G. Hunt, eds. *Impact of Racism on White Americans.* Newbury Park, Calif.: Sage Publications, 1981.

A series of twelve papers by sociologists and psychologists focusing on how racism in America is created, maintained, and condoned by a white majority. Describes the impact of racism on education, employment, religion, and government. 288 pages with an index.

Caditz, Judith. *White Liberals in Transition: Current Dilemmas of Ethnic Integration.* New York: Spectrum Publications, 1976.

A challenge to the view that the major source of opposition to integration is among working-class and poorly educated whites. Many white middle-class liberals are inconsistent in their support for breaking down the barriers of color. They support it in principle but fail to take any action that would bring about any significant change. 187 pages with and index.

Campbell, Angus. *White Attitudes Toward Black People.* Ann Arbor, Mich.: Institute for Social Research, 1971.

Analysis of a fifteen-city study for the National Advisory Commission on Civil Disorders (the Kerner Commission). A majority of whites held racist attitudes and were resistant to any major change in race relations. One positive result: those whites who attended college were less likely to express racist ideas. 177 pages.

Campbell, Ernest Q. *Racial Tensions and National Identity.* Nashville: Vanderbilt University Press, 1972.

Papers from the Second Annual Vanderbilt Sociology Conference, 1970. Eight essays on racial problems in England, the United States, Rhodesia, Brazil, South Africa, Africa, and Malaysia. Discussions of power, privilege, protest, control, response, and types of accommodation. H. Hoetink's essay, "National Identity, Culture, and Race in the Caribbean" (pages 17-42), is especially enlightening. 259 pages with an index.

Cherry, Robert. *Discrimination: Its Impact on Blacks, Women, and Jews.* Lexington, Mass.: Lexington Books, 1989.

A useful book, by an economist, that examines the contrasting theories of the costs of discrimination. Written for nonspecialists, it presents liberal and conservative views and provides students with a nonpartisan summary of the problems. 235 pages with eighteen tables and an index.

Parsons, Talcott, and Kenneth B. Clark, eds. *The Negro American.* Boston: Beacon Press, 1966.

A collection of essays by leading historians, sociologists, and psychologists. These essays helped provide background information for War on Poverty programs. 314 pages with an index.

Cohen, Carl. *Naked Racial Preference.* Lanham, Md.: Madison Books, 1995.

An attack on affirmative action. Includes a discussion of nine Supreme Court cases concerning race relations and the Constitution. Cohen argues that race should not be used for anyone's advantage in employment, education, or the delivery of public goods. 242 pages.

Coles, Robert. *Children in Crisis: A Study in Courage and Fear.* Boston: Little, Brown, 1967.

Presents the famous psychiatrist's perspective on the heroic role played by black children in the struggle against segregation. Describes the psychological costs of discrimination and how it impoverishes the soul.

Cottingham, Clement, ed. *Race, Poverty, and the Urban Underclass.* Lexington, Mass.: Lexington Books, 1982.

Nine essays on the growth of what some social commentators have called the underclass. The focus is on the relationship between race and poverty in America's cities. Tries to answer the question of why poverty continues to exist in the richest nation in the history of the world. Also provides an evaluation of some successful government programs aimed at fighting poverty. 208 pages with notes.

Crouch, Stanley. *The All-American Skin Game: Or, The Decoy of Race: The Long and Short of It, 1990-1994.* New York: Pantheon Books, 1995.
Essays on music, racism, and motion pictures by a noted jazz critic. Includes a tribute to Ralph Ellison and his contributions to literature and culture, especially

Davis, Allison, and John Dollard. *Children of Bondage.* New York: Harper & Row, 1964.
A classic examination of the psychological and social damage done to children in a society dominated by beliefs in white superiority. A useful reminder of the effects of hatred on the personalities and belief systems of those who have been victimized by hate-filled ideas.

Dorn, Edwin. *Rules and Racial Equality.* New Haven, Conn.: Yale University Press, 1979.
In the United States, there are elaborate justifications supporting inequality. For example, most Americans believe in the rule that "everybody has an equal right to opportunity." Nothing follows about whether everybody has had equal "opportunity." All that follows is that if anyone has a right to it, "no one has a greater or less right than he." Thus, the rule is fair and the results, no matter how unequal, are also fair. The failure to define opportunity has had tragic consequences for millions of citizens. 155 pages with an index.

Dovido, John F. and Samuel L. Gaertner. *Prejudice, Discrimination, and Racism.* Orlando: Academic Press, 1986.
Papers on the motivational, cognitive, social and cultural factors involved in the development of racist attitudes. These eleven essays describe the historical trends in racism, the ways racist ideas are acquired, the different forms of racism, and the consequences of racist ideas in schools, courtrooms, and businesses. Most of the essays are by psychologists and sociologists and are aimed at graduate students. 337 pages with an index.

D'Souza, Dinesh. *The End of Racism: Principles for a Multicultural Society.* New York: Free Press, 1995.
Perhaps the only book in this bibliography that denies that racism ever led to anything bad in American history. Hopeful but not well grounded in history. 736 pages with an index.

Dunbar, Leslie W. *Minority Report: What Has Happened to Blacks, American Indians, and Other Minorities in the Eighties.* New York: Pantheon Books, 1984.

Essays by journalists, sociologists, and civil rights leaders assessing the damage done to civil rights by the first Reagan Administration. Describes the attack on affirmative action, the abuse of the criminal justice system in which a "war on crime" results in a war to incapacitate young black males, and the regrowth of poverty. 236 pages with an index.

Farley, Reynolds. *Blacks and Whites: Narrowing the Gap?* Cambridge, Mass.: Harvard University Press, 1984.

Finds mixed progress in jobs and education. Racism is not dead although there has been some progress as a result of federal government efforts. The greatest threat to further gains for African Americans would be a major economic depression and a federal administration that gave low priority to racial justice. 235 pages with an index.

Farley, Reynolds, and Walter R. Allen. *The Color Line and the Quality of Life in America.* New York: Russell Sage Foundation, 1987.

A massive work of research based on U.S. Census Bureau figures comparing the economic and social status of white and black Americans. Describes the relationship, over time, in family structure, fertility, mortality, migration, education, and income. Finds the reality of discrimination based on race stills lies heavy on African Americans. White America is to blame because it has had the major responsibility for denying equal opportunity to people of color. 493 pages with figures, tables, and an index.

Flynt, J. Wayne. *Dixie's Forgotten People: The South's Poor Whites.* Bloomington: Indiana University Press, 1979.

Focuses on the period after 1945 and the experience of an economically exploited, politically abused people: poor white southerners. They had few tools to improve their own lives and only one source of pride—their race. This study of their culture, religion, and music describes the limited lives and opportunities of the least educated members of the white majority. 206 pages with a bibliography and an index.

_____. *Poor But Proud: Alabama's Poor Whites.* Tuscaloosa: University of Alabama Press, 1989.

An updated but more specialized study of the author's first work. Especially good in analyzing the influence of religion on poor white society. An updated bibliography and an index.

Goldschmid, Marcel L., ed. *Black Americans and White Racism: Theory and Research.* New York: Holt, Rinehart and Winston, 1970.
Descriptions of research findings from the 1960's by eminent scholars in the field. Each essay introduced by the editor. Includes work on black identity and personality; the black family; race and intellectual performance; black achievement in a segregated culture; the sources of prejudice and discrimination, and the growth of militancy and violence. 434 pages with tables, graphs, and an index.

Guinier, Lani. *The Tyranny of the Majority: Fundamental Fairness in a Representative Democracy.* New York: Free Press, 1994.
A review of voting discrimination laws and a call for reform that includes cumulative voting to break the tyranny of the majority. By the legal scholar nominated and then withdrawn by President Clinton for Assistant Attorney General for Civil Rights. 324 pages with an index.

Gwaltney, John L. *Drylongo: A Self-Portrait of Black Americans.* New York: Random House, 1980.
The product of an anthropological field study done in the early 1970's in a dozen unnamed northeastern, urban, African American communities. Includes personal narratives and descriptions of life in poor and middle-class society. A rare look at black culture as perceived by African Americans. 287 pages.

Hendin, Herbert. *Black Suicide.* New York: Basic Books, 1969.
A major study by a psychiatrist of the causes of suicide in the African American community. Emphasizes the role of social factors such as crime, drug addiction, and family abuse in the lives of black teenagers, the one group that has a suicide rate as high as that of whites. In all other age groups, the rate for African Americans is much less than that of whites. From the perspective of the late 1960's, it predicts an increase in suicide in the black community, and this has turned out to be correct. A frightening look at people being acted upon by others who are way beyond any individual's ability to control.

Hentoff, Nat, ed. *Black Anti-Semitism and Jewish Racism.* New York: Richard W. Baron, 1969.
A collection of essays by writers such as James Baldwin, Harold Cruse, Julius Lester, and others on an issue that has received wide attention. What is the cause of African American hatred of Jews? Baldwin answers that blacks "are anti-Semitic because they're anti-white." Along with white policemen, Jews are the only whites (or used to be until they sold their stores to Koreans) generally visible in African

American communities. Many of them tend to be successful, by ghetto standards, and thus they are hated. 237 pages.

Hernton, Calvin C. *Sex and Racism.* Garden City, N.Y.: Grove Press, 1965.
An angry work by an African American poet and social scientist. Suggests that all race relations tend to be "sex relations." Discusses the history of sexual involvement between whites and blacks from slavery days to the early 1960's. Racism has been used by whites to distort and deprave the humanity of Africans mainly to keep black men away from white women. 180 pages.

Hill, Robert B., ed. *Research on the African-American Family: A Holistic Perspective.* Westport, Conn.: Auburn House, 1993.
A review of recent social and economic trends among African Americans. Includes essays on the widening gap between black and white incomes; causes of out-of-wedlock births among black women, and the increase in poverty in the 1980's in African American families. 195 pages with a bibliography and an index.

Holden, Matthew. *The White Man's Burden.* New York: Chandler Publishing, 1973.
Essays on the growing racial schism in the United States by a white civil rights activist and political scientist. Will white America develop the capacity to accept measures which would break racism? Speculates that this is unlikely and suggests this eventually will lead to a race war. 284 pages with an index.

Holloway, Karla F. *Codes of Conduct: Race, Ethics, and the Color of Our Character.* New Brunswick, N.J.: Rutgers University Press, 1995.
Nine essays of cultural criticism by a literary critic. A challenging but often frustrating collection.

Jaynes, Gerald D., and Robin M. Williams, Jr., eds. *A Common Destiny: Blacks and American Society.* Washington, D.C.: National Academy Press, 1989.
A huge collection of data, essays, historical documents, and studies by social scientists on every aspect of African American life. Includes sections on history, politics, attitudes and behavior, social structure, economics, education, health care, crime and justice, and children and families. Hundreds of charts, tables, and diagrams. 607 pages with an index.

Jencks, Christopher. *Rethinking Social Policy: Race, Poverty, and the Underclass.* Cambridge, Mass.: Harvard University Press, 1992.
Provides a brief history of recent social policy and five other essay by the author on the central questions dividing liberal and conservative policy makers. Critically analyzes the positions advanced by Thomas Sowell, Charles Murray, and William Julius Wilson. A very useful presentation of data and ideas. 280 pages with an index.

Kardiner, Abram, and Lionel Ovesey. *The Mark of Oppression: A Psychosocial Study of the American Negro.* New York: W. W. Norton, 1951.
A classic study of the effects of racism on those being acted upon by the racist majority. Reminds readers that prejudice and discrimination do influence the way people think about themselves and others.

Katz, Irwin, and Patricia Gurin, eds. *Race and the Social Sciences.* New York: Basic Books, 1969.
An interesting collection of essays providing an interdisciplinary approach to race relations. Includes research by sociologists, psychologists, political scientists, and economists. A call for more research into the causes of racial conflict and discrimination. 387 pages with notes and an index.

Kaus, Mickey. *The End of Equality.* New York: Basic Books, 1992.
An attack on the welfare state by a former liberal. Sees an America separated by social class. Calls for a program of job creation to replace welfare, supporting the idea of "billions for worker, not a penny for welfare." Does not examine the problem of child labor. 293 pages with note and an index.

Keegan, Frank L. *Blacktown, U.S.A.* Boston: Little, Brown, 1971.
A white journalist interviews residents of African American communities in order to help whites realize what they have done to blacks through racism and discrimination. 428 pages with photographs.

Kinder, Donald, and Lynn M. Sanders. *Divided by Color: Racial Politics and Democratic Ideas.* Chicago: University of Chicago Press, 1996.
Presents a survey of attitudes along the racial divide. Black and white Americans look upon question of social policy in entirely different and, to each other, unintelligible ways. They have a terrible time talking to one another about race or anything else. 391 pages with notes and an index.

Knopke, Harry J., and Robert J. Norrell. *Opening Doors: Perspectives on Race Relations in Contemporary America.* Tuscaloosa: University of Alabama Press, 1991.

Papers from a symposium held in 1988 on the occasion of the twenty-fifth anniversary of Governor George Wallace's standing in the door of the University of Alabama to block the registration of two African American students. The best essay is Mortimer Ostow's "A Psychoanalytical Approach to the Problems of Prejudice and Persecution" (pages 79-99). Prejudice is a mechanism for resolving conflicts acquired early in life (for example, sibling rivalry). Undesirable thoughts resulting from this prejudice are then projected upon scapegoats and outgroups. 234 pages with an index.

Knowles, Louis L., and Kenneth Prewitt, eds. *Institutional Racism in America.* Englewood Cliffs, N.J.: Prentice-Hall, 1969.

Written by two white teachers who lived and worked in an African American community, this work describes racism in American businesses and economic life. It includes essays concerning the substandard education of African American children, the miseducation of whites, and the pervasiveness of racism in the American legal and judicial system. 180 pages with an index.

Kochman, Thomas. *Black and White Styles in Conflict.* Chicago: University of Chicago Press, 1981.

Black language and culture is much different than white language and culture. Contacts at school and work lead to significant misconceptions and hostilities based on lack of understanding. 177 pages with an index.

Kotlowitz, Alex. *There Are No Children Here: The Story of Two Boys Growing Up in the Other America.* New York: Doubleday, 1991.

The best recent portrait of life in the ghetto. The story of life in a Chicago housing project as seen by two young residents. Must reading for anyone concerned about race relations in the United States. 324 pages with an index.

Kovel, Joel. *White Racism: A Psychohistory.* New York: Pantheon Books, 1970.

Far from being the simple delusion of a bigoted and ignorant minority, racism results from a set of beliefs whose structure comes from the deepest levels of our minds and lives, from the very way people are taught to understand the world. Racism is part of humans' fantasy explanation of how the world works. 300 pages with an index.

Kozol, Jonathan. *Amazing Grace: The Lives of Children and the Conscience of a Nation.* New York: Crown Publishers, 1995.
Kozol observed children growing up in the South Bronx, noting how they lived, died, and survived. He chronicles a year in their lives, describing the effects of racism, poverty, and Reaganism. 286 pages with an index.

————. *Death at an Early Age: The Destruction of the Hearts and Minds of Negro Children in the Boston Public Schools.* Boston: Houghton Mifflin, 1967.
The author spent a year teaching in a Boston public school. He documents the problems, fears, and discriminations experienced by his students. A strong call for action issued before Americans started blaming the kids themselves for their difficulties. 246 pages.

Larkins, John R. *Alcohol and the Negro: Explosive Issues.* Zebulon, N.C.: Record Publishing, 1965.
A history by a black social scientist of the effects of alcohol on African American religion, economics, and politics. Sees alcohol abuse as part of a system of social control foisted upon blacks by whites. Alcoholism in also a protest against the treatment accorded African Americans in the dominant political and economic structure of society. Social conditions in black communities foster frustration and the desire to escape. In the period before illegal drugs were introduced into American society on a massive scale, alcohol served as the primary escape from the burdens of daily living. 251 pages with notes.

Levitan, Sar A., William B. Johnston, and Robert Taggart. *Still a Dream: The Changing Status of Blacks Since 1960.* Cambridge, Mass.: Harvard University Press, 1975.
This study finds some progress in economic status, but little progress in social equality, education for the majority of African Americans, or job opportunities.

Lyman, Stanford. *The Black American in Sociological Thought.* New York: G. P. Putnam's Sons, 1972.
A critical review of the thought of the Social Darwinists, Robert E. Park, Gunnar Myrdal, Talcott Parsons, and various psychological theories of prejudice. Finds that social thought has been dominated by a view of slow, orderly motion and progress. This ignores history which follows a path of crisis and catastrophe. Change occurs but it is irregular and discontinuous. It is sometimes based on chance, violence, or war—not simply on men of good will acting together in concert. The

author's views do not seem to have had much impact on contemporary social thought. 220 pages with notes and an index.

Massey, Douglas S., and Nancy A. Denton. *American Apartheid: Segregation and the Making of the Underclass.* Cambridge, Mass.: Harvard University Press, 1993.
Describes the consequences of segregation. It is the key feature of American society responsible for the perpetuation of urban poverty and is the a primary cause of racial inequality. Segregation has produced the disadvantaged neighborhood environment responsible for creation of the underclass. The ghetto can only be dismantled with strict enforcement of fair housing laws. 292 pages with notes, charts, tables, and an index.

Moses, Wilson Jeremiah. *The Wings of Ethiopia: Studies in African-American Life and Letters.* Ames: Iowa State University Press, 1990.
Essays written between 1969 and 1989 by a key black sociologist. Includes his observations on black nationalism, religion, intellectual life, slavery, literature, and the Civil Rights movement. 291 pages with an index.

Olzak, Susan. *The Dynamics of Ethnic Competition and Conflict.* Stanford, Calif.: Stanford University Press, 1992.
Explores various models of racial confrontation. Finds that group conflict increases when barriers to ethnic contact and competition begin to break down. Desegregation efforts always cause conflict with the violence directed toward those least able to retaliate, the elderly, women, and children. 271 pages with an index.

Pinkney, Alphonso. *The Myth of Black Progress.* New York: Cambridge University Press, 1984.
According to Pinkney, racism is less openly displayed in 1984 than in 1964, but it continues to oppress people and is an ever-present part of the American way of life. 198 pages with an index.

Porter, Judith D. R. *Black Child, White Child: The Development of Racial Attitudes.* Cambridge, Mass.: Harvard University Press, 1971.
An important book that describes the genesis of racism and prejudice among whites and the effects such attitudes have on very young African American children. 278 pages with notes, tables, and an index.

Rainwater, Lee. *Behind Ghetto Walls: Black Families in a Federal Slum.* Chicago: Aldine Publishing, 1970.

Describes how life was lived in the recently destroyed Pruitt-Igoe housing project in St. Louis. Written by a sociologist who explains the impact of inequality and racism on the lives of the project's inhabitants. 446 pages with an index.

Reddy, Maureen T. *Crossing the Color Line: Race, Parenting, and Culture.* New Brunswick, N.J.: Rutgers University Press, 1994.
An autobiographical narrative by a white mother of black children who is also a professor of English. Reddy talks about trying to understand the meaning of race and about the meeting points of whiteness and blackness. 193 pages with an index.

Reich, Michael. *Racial Inequality: A Political-Economic Analysis.* Princeton, N.J.: Princeton University Press, 1981.
An economic history of racial inequality since 1865. Finds that racial inequality had greatly benefited rich white Americans. For poorer whites, it is a different story; racism has divided workers and kept wages down. It has been used by corporations to increase profits, in places where unionization has been lower and racial inequality greater profits have been higher. Racism plays a useful role in a capitalist society, because it provides a scapegoat (blacks) upon whom the frustrations and failures of one's own life can be blamed. 345 pages with tables, figures, and an index.

Rice, Mitchell F., and Woodrow Jones, Jr., eds. *Contemporary Public Policy Perspectives and Black Americans: Issues in an Era of Retrenchment Politics.* Westport, Conn.: Greenwood Press, 1984.
Original essays on the effects of welfare policy in the early Reagan years. Discussions of the urban crisis, public employment, minority businesses, energy, the military, the police, affirmative action, health care, and the future. Cutbacks and block grants for health care, for instance, tend to make things much worse. Policies based on state and local government powers will re-create pre-1964 conditions in the United States. 209 pages with charts, notes, and an index.

Rooney, Robert C. *Equal Opportunity in the United States: A Symposium on Civil Rights.* Austin, Tex.: Lyndon B. Johnson School of Public Affairs. 1973.
Speeches and observations from a civil rights symposium which included Earl Warren, Hubert Humphrey, Vernon Jordan, Roy Wilkins, Julian Bond, and Burke Marshall. Humphrey summarized the problems by remarking, "We are climbing a molasses mountain dressed in snowshoes." 175 pages.

Ross, Arthur M., and Herbert Hill, eds. *Employment, Race, and Poverty: A Critical Study of the Disadvantaged Status of Negro Workers from 1865 to 1965.* New York: Harcourt, Brace & World, 1967.

A massive compilation of statistical evidence pointing to the great advantages enjoyed by whites workers in a racially segregated economic and social system. Essays on the social effects of unemployment, the impact of unions, and the importance of education and training. Produced by the Research Program on Unemployment and the American Economy at the University of California, Berkeley. 598 pages with tables, charts, and an index.

Schuman, Howard, and Shirley Hatchett. *Black Racial Attitudes: Trends and Complexities.* Ann Arbor: Institute for Social Research, University of Michigan, 1974.

A study based on public opinion surveys. Very enlightening and upsetting, or at least the findings should be to whites.

Shull, Steven A. *The President and Civil Rights Policy: Leadership and Change.* New York: Greenwood Press, 1989.

A comparison of presidents from Lyndon Johnson to Ronald Reagan concerning their views of civil rights enforcement. Finds that a president can make his policy preferences prevail, either by doing something or doing nothing. Also includes a study of the media's role in promoting civil rights. 251 pages with tables, notes, and an index.

Sigelmen, Lee, and Susan Welch. *Black Americans' Views of Racial Inequality.* New York: Cambridge University Press, 1991.

An analysis of opinions from the late 1980's. Finds that 25 percent of African Americans think a majority of whites accept policies of the Ku Klux Klan. They experience white hostility almost daily and many see limited, halting gains for themselves while they believe whites are making rapid economic advances. 214 pages with tables and an index.

Smith, J. Owens. *The Politics of Racial Inequality: A Systematic Comparative Macro-Analysis from the Colonial Period to 1970.* Westport, Conn.: Greenwood Press, 1987.

Written by a professor of political science, this work explores the reasons why African Americans have been unable to escape from the slums. White racism as expressed in their political attitudes and views is the most important factor. African Americans never received the same help as did Europeans, even the Homestead Act discriminated against blacks. 202 pages with notes and an index.

Sonenshein, Raphael J. *Politics in Black and White: Race and Power in Los Angeles.* Princeton, N.J.: Princeton University Press, 1993.

Can whites and minorities find common ground for political organization? The evidence is mixed in this study of Los Angeles politics from 1960 to 1990 written by a political scientist. Leadership is most important, since biracial coalitions can work only with dedicated leaders who share common goals of power, justice, and equality. 301 pages with an index.

Southern, David W. *Gunnar Myrdal and Black-White Relations: The Use and Abuse of an American Dilemma, 1944-1969.* Baton Rouge: Louisiana State University Press, 1987.

A study of how Myrdal's ideas got into people's heads, especially social scientists and political leaders. Myrdal made an optimistic view of race relations possible. If whites began to feel guilty enough about how they treated African Americans, conditions could begin to improve. White guilt was a necessary ingredient for change. 341 pages with notes, a select bibliography, and an index.

Spickard, Paul R. *Mixed Blood: Intermarriage and Ethnic Identity in Twentieth Century America.* Madison: University of Wisconsin Press, 1989.

An analysis of Japanese, Jewish, and African American interracial marriages. Finds that those people most emancipated from their ethnic and racial heritage are most likely to intermarry. Americans, however, see race as a much greater barrier between people than religion or ethnicity. 532 pages with notes, a bibliography, and an index.

Stember, Charles Herbert. *Sexual Racism: The Emotional Barrier to Integrated Society.* New York: Elsevier Scientific Publishing, 1968. Reprint. New York: Elsevier, 1976.

Emotions surrounding sexual attraction produce great hostilities toward African Americans and puts strong barriers in the way of achieving equality. Based on interviews and a reading of the literature on race relations. 234 pages with an index.

Sniderman, Paul M., and Michael G. Hagen. *Race and Inequality: A Study in American Values.* Chatham, N.J.: Chatham House, 1985.

Americans are extreme individualists who judge all people on their own terms. Most Americans believe that everyone can make it if they simply try hard enough. They are radical egalitarians who minimize the problems of prejudice and discrimination. A very useful study of white attitudes toward inequality and how this accounts for the persistence of racism. 158 pages with an index.

Thomas, Alexander and Samuel Sillen. *Racism and Psychiatry.* New York: Brunner/Mazel Publishers, 1972.
Examines the ways in which white racism has influenced the theory and practice of psychiatry by two psychiatrists. Includes a useful summary of the racist ideas that influenced professional and popular writers in the field. 176 pages with an index.

Thurow, Lester C. *Poverty and Discrimination.* Washington, 1969.
A study of how one leads to the other. A short, highly interesting book by a leading economist. 178 pages with an index.

Tucker, M. Belinda, and Claudia Mitchell-Kennan, eds. *The Decline in Marriage Among African Americans: Causes, Consequences, and Policy Implications.* New York: Russell Sage Foundation, 1990.
Links the decline to a drop in the pool of marriageable black males. Takes a look at the effects of economic instability and job loss on the black community. 416 pages with an index.

Wellman, David T. *Portraits of White Racism.* New York: Cambridge University Press, 1993.
Too many white Americans have become smug and complacent and finds that currently racism is minimized by many people. Includes five case studies based on in-depth interviews of white people. Much evidence that prejudice continues to play a major role in American society. Although crime rates for aggravated assault are the same regardless of race, the proportion of blacks arrested for that category of crime is three times higher than that for whites. At the same time, even though African Americans represent only about 20 percent of the nation's drug users, they constitute more than two-thirds of the population arrested. 270 pages with an index.

West, Cornel. *Race Matters.* Boston: Beacon Press, 1993.
Essays by a professor of religion that explore his experiences with discrimination and his hopes for America. West calls for a new language of empathy and compassion, or more fire will come. 105 pages.

Wicker, Tom. *Tragic Failure: Racial Integration in America.* New York: William Morrow, 1996.
The pessimistic conclusions of a noted *New York Times* journalist. Neither the Civil War nor the Civil Rights movement produced equal-

ity, unity, or racial peace. Racism will never be overcome, according to Wicker, because white feelings of superiority depend on black oppression. 218 pages with notes and an index.

Willie, Charles Vert. *The Ivory and Ebony Towers: Race Relations and Higher Education.* Lexington, Mass.: Lexington Books, 1981.
A comparative study of black and white students to each other and to their teachers. Education is liberation. Supports a philosophy that emphasizes adequacy rather than excellence. Excellence is a individual goal toward which students should aspire. Society should demand of education, however, that it create astute, adequately literate graduates who can help solve society's problems. This is preferable to a system in which only a few of its members are educated for excellence. 173 pages with tables and an index.

_____. *Oreo: On Race and Marginal Men and Women.* Wakefield, Mass.: Parameter Press, 1975.
African Americans are a marginal people in America with a mission not unlike that of Jewish people in the Old World: They will lead Americans to salvation and redemption. 95 pages with an index.

Wilson, William Julius. *The Declining Significance of Race: Blacks and Changing American Institutions.* Chicago: University of Chicago Press, 1978.
Sees race declining as an influence in American economic and social life just at a time when in reality in seemed to be reemerging as a key factor. Reinforces the view that blacks are responsible for their own position in society. Wilson's view is that, despite evidence to the contrary, affirmative action cannot help blacks.

AUTHOR INDEX

SUBJECT INDEX

About the Author

Leslie Vincent Tischauser is a professor of history and chair of the Department of Social Science at Prairie State Community College in Chicago Heights, Illinois, where he teaches American and world history. His research area is the twentieth century United States, emphasizing ethnic and political history. He is a former member of Volunteers in Service to America (VISTA). He has previously published *The German Question in Chicago, 1914-1941* (1990), and is at work on another book, *Black History for White Americans*. He is also a member of the history faculty at Roosevelt University, Chicago, where he teaches a course on the history of Chicago, and at Governors State University, University Park, Illinois, where he presents courses in European history.